ANTHROPOLOGY OF TOURISM
A Case Study of Chitwan-Sauraha, Nepal

ANTHROPOLOGY OF TOURISM

A Case Study of Chitwan-Sauraha, Nepal

Ramesh Raj Kunwar

ADROIT PUBLISHERS
Delhi-110 053

Published by
ADROIT PUBLISHERS
C-8/2, Yamuna Vihar, Delhi-110 053
Phone: 3266030, 3242552

Distributors
AKHIL BOOK DISTRIBUTORS
4675/21, Ganpati Bhawan, Ansari Road,
Darya Ganj, New Delhi-110 002
Phones : 3266030, 3242552
e-mail: akhilbooks@yahoo.com

ISBN : 81-87392-34-7

Layout by
Sudhir Kumar Vatsa

Laser Typeset by
Nidhi Laser Point
e-mail: nidhi_vatsa@hotmail.com

Printed in India on behalf of M/s Adroit Publishers by
Arpit Printographers, B-7, Saraswati Complex,
Subhash Chowk, Laxmi Nagar, Delhi-110 092

ACKNOWLEDGEMENTS

In this kind of study, the researcher has to encounter with several people who are directly or indirectly associated with this work. In this connection, I met Bishnu Sharma, an experienced naturalist, Daya Man Dangol of Chitwan Resort Camp, Sukhai Chaudhari, Mclean Joan (the Australian lady), the authorities of King Mahendra Trust, Gyanendra Prasad Khatiwoda of Hotel Hermitage, B.P. Chaudhari and Giridhari Chaudhari of Sauraha. I express my sincere thanks to all those people of Sauraha.

Linda K. Ritcher (2000:vii) writes, "Authoring a book is rather like having a baby, in that it needs the cooperation of others, involves a certain amount of anxiety and discomfort, and rarely leaves one in the same mental or physical shape that they were in before. Unlike producing a baby, the gestation period is longer, the cooperation needed more sustained and varied, and the end result a bit anticlimatic."

In research of this kind the collection of primary data is of crucial significance. Hence I express my sincere thanks to all naturalist friends, hoteliers of Sauraha and other Tharu respondents of Sauraha, Odra, Patna, Dhindauli and Marchauli villages of Bachhauli Village Development Committee and Padampur VDC.

If Prof. Dr. Ram Niwas Pandey had not brought the project from UNESCO in 1992, I would not be in a position to work in Sauraha Chitwan. I would be failing in my duty, if I do not mention his name in this book. Two persons who deserve a special mention are Prof. Lionel Caplan, then Head of the Department of Anthropology at SOAS (in 1990), London, and Dr. Yehudi Gordon, an eminent gynecologist of Golders Green of north London, who not only provided me facility to work on anthropology of tourism at SOAS but also facilitated lodging and fooding respectively. My equal thanks go to Prof. Dr. Prem Raman Upreti, an eminent historian of Nepal, and Prof. Dr. Mukunda Raj Aryal, the Head of the Department of Culture, Tribhuvan University.

If Dr. Gita Khadka had not seen the part of this manuscript, my effort could be of no use. Therefore, I express my sincere thanks to Dr. Gita Khadka, Associate Professor of Department of English. Similar thanks goes to Yoga Raj Gautam, the lecturer of Nobel college, Kathmandu.

It is Prof. Dr. Abhi Subedi who provided me an opportunity to read a synopsis of this book at the International Folklore Congress held in Kathmandu, 2001. Hence I convey my most grateful thanks to Prof. Dr. Abhi Subedi.

I should not forget to acknowledge Sharad Chandra Shah, Mr. Pawan Tuladhar and Sunil Bajracharya of Dharma Adventure (Travels and Trekking Agency), Sambhu Pathak of Blue Bird Travel Agency, Surya Prakash Shrestha of OM Travels and Tours, Dibya Shahi and Kusum Shahi of Daina Travel Agency and Ang Phurba Sherpa of Wilderness Experience Trekking Agency.

It is Anil Ratna Tuladhar (the Managing Director of Tika Travels and Tours) who always encouraged me to complete this work as soon as possible. Therefore, I express my thanks to him. In course of writing this book, I got a lot of help from Mandala Book Point. Therefore, I sincerely thank to Bidur Dangol and all his family members.

I am extremely indebted to my closest friend Madhav Lal Maharjan for providing some excellent pictures, specially the picture of Rhino mating. I express deep gratitude to D.K. Sharma of Adroit Publishers for his kind help in bringing out this book in a span of very short time.

Finally my sincere thanks go to Mr. Prashanna Shrestha, Sudarshan Khadka, Ramhari Khadka, Surendra Raut, Rajat Thapa and Surya Singh Thapa of Mac Support for the help in excellent computer settings and support of other facilities.

PREFACE

The world is getting smaller inside every day due to the rapid advancement of transport and communication and man's life is getting busier in a closed, stereotyped and monotonous society. Man by nature cannot live in confinement. He seeks change to invigorate himself from time to time. He is always tempted to experience a new taste of life in the exotic society. A modern man can live in a modest living but he cannot forsake his habit of travelling and hence, his interest of knowing something new. Consequently tourism has developed astronomically throughout the world.

A country not only earns foreign exchange and provides jobs and employment, it also fulfills the basic needs, provides comforts and modern amenities to locals and corrects regional disparities by developing various infrastructures for tourism. For sustainable tourism development the quintessential factor is political stability and peace. If there is no peace and political stability, no beautiful road, efficient communication, air service, health, sanitation, cleanliness and hygienic food, fresh air, water quality, natural and cultural history and manufactured heritage, proper planning and policies carrying capacity can motivate the tourists because the destination is politically disturbed through internal and conventional war. In that case the question is automatically raised how sustained is sustainable? Another important feature of tourism is time.

The tourists are very much concerned with time. For them time is more important than money. They do not mind paying money. Even in vacation their activities have to be completed within a particular time frame because they have to go back to their country to join their usual work. In the third world the term sustainable tourism development has become very popular but there it is not realized that for the tourist time is money and money is development. Time is also service. Service is a product and the product has satisfy to the tourists. If there is no prompt service, there will be no quality tourists. Regarding service in the context of tourism there are found two sayings: T(ourists) are like so many cattle, representing highly mobile, productive, and prestigious, but perishable, forms of wealth. Like cattle, tourists give good milk, but only if they are well fed (Fisher, 1990:123). First the cows leave, then the guests—who should we milk now? (Krippendorf, 1984:434, cited in Price, 1995:207).

Tourism is motivated by Sunlust (pull) and Wanderlust (push), also described as man's nature of seeking and escaping. These days tourism is also looked upon as a means of meeting personal needs and resolving interpersonal problems, and more efficient means of transportation. However, consequences and impacts are on both the hosts and the guests. The host–guest relationship is unique and full of unbalanced experiences. If for the guest, the relationship is unique, the meeting is fascinating for the host. It is merely one of many superficial relationships, experienced throughout the tourist season. For the host the tourist season is another kind of festival in which the individuals of the destination area will not only be busy in earning money but will also be busy in making fun with the tourist.

In the case of Nepal, the ancestors of Nepalese people were not unfamiliar with the term *paryatan* (going out for pleasure and knowledge), *deshatan* (visiting abroad primarily for economic gain), *tirthatan* (traveling abroad for religious merit), *akhet* (hunting) and *vihara* (excursions). These days we are familiar with the term leisure and pleasure. This reveals that tourism in Nepal is already recognised as an instrument for development. Despite some progress over the past few decades we have failed to eradicate poverty and remove inequitable access to the resources required for better living—education, health services and income source.

Nepal is a tourist receiving country where 491,684 tourists visited in 1999 and 463,646 visited in 2000. For tourism development and promotion we need to go with four major platforms (advocacy platform, cautionary platform, adaptancy platform and knowledge-based platform) suggested by the eminent Prof. Jafar Jafari. Nepalese planners, policy makers, professionals, development agents, concerning authorities, politicians, and students of travel and tourism must think very seriously about the political instability and internal disorder. Now Nepal without tourism is condemned but with tourism culture is destroyed. The solution is cultural tourism (to be developed) along with adventure tourism (already existing). Cultural tourism is a balance phenomenon for both the hosts and guests. No matter whether tourism is an industry or a social phenomenon different professionals, researchers and planners have given different connotations from the view point of industry. It is said that tourism is a smokeless industry, people industry, vacation industry, decentralised industry, service industry, multifaceted industry and legitimate industry. Whichever industry it is, the entrepreneurs take it as a golden goose that lays golden eggs and the others see the goose fouls in the nest which should be cleaned for sustainable tourism development. I have made an effort to introduce anthropology of tourism, a new area in the academic field of tourism. I hope this will be very useful to the students of anthropology, sociology and other disciplines, policy makers, planners, researchers, development agents, marketers and other general readers for understanding the inter cultural interconnection between the hosts and the guests. Equal efforts have been made to provide a wealth of information, ideas, knowledge and theories to the readers. From academic perspectives, tourism is considered as social science.

An effort has been made to analyse the ways in which tourism is contributing to changes in value systems, individual behaviour, family relationships, ethics and moral conduct, creative expressions, traditional/ceremonies, community organizations as they are in the process of trivialisation, revitalisation, trinketisation and cocacolisation.

The evolution of tourism education is presented, and the suggestion is made that tourism thinking has passed through two distinct stages:

(1) the early 1940s–1970s, characterised by pragmatic concerns of educators for such things as career preparation and placement and

(2) beginning in the early 1980s, a shift from the pragmatic to the academic, emphasising research and methods of inquiry.

However, the 1990s are seen as a period of transformation brought about by social change, concern for the environment, a global economy and rapid advancement in technology (Theobald, 1997:310).

For greater recognition, emphasis should probably be given to the role of tourism in applied anthropology, and the growing interface between industry and academia. Esoteric studies on the nature of tourist motivations for travel have direct applications in marketing strategies. The use of mitigation techniques to resolve conflict between hosts and guests, non-national managers and native employees, and land-use planners and environmentalists augurs well for greater professionalism in tourism management. Many travel industry conferences regularly schedule one or two sessions on tourism research as part of their format, and anthropologists, geographers and psychologists thus find employment as industry consultants (Smith, 1989:XI).

Dr. Ramesh Raj Kunwar

CONTENTS

Chapter One

DEFINITION OF TOURISM

Etymologically, the word tour is derived from the Latin 'tornare' and the Greek 'tornos', meaning 'a lathe or circle; the movement around a central point or axis'. This meaning changed in modern English to represent 'one's turn'. The suffix 'ism' is defined as 'an action or process; typical behavior or quality', while the suffix 'ist' denotes 'one that performs a given action'. When the word tour and the suffixes 'ism' and 'ist' are combined, they suggest the action of movement around a circle. One can argue that circle represents a starting point, which ultimately returns to its beginning. Therefore, like a circle, a tour represents a journey that it is a round-trip, i.e., the act of leaving and then returning to the original starting point, and therefore, one who takes such a journey can be called a tourist (Theobald, 1997:6).

The most widely accepted, but technical, definition of the tourist was proposed by the International Union of Official Travel Organizations (IUOTO) in 1963 and approved in 1968 by the World Tourist Organization (Leiper 1979:393). It states that (international) tourists are 'temporary visitors staying at least twenty-four hours in the country visited and the purpose of whose journey can be classified under one of the following headings:

(a) leisure (recreation, holiday, health, study, religion and sport);

(b) business (family mission, meeting)' (IUOTO 1963:14). This

> definition is useful primarily for 'statistical, legislative and industrial purposes' (Burkart and Medlik 1974:3), but it is unsatisfactory for most sociological work because it is too broad and theoretically barren.

The word tourism, for example, is capable of diverse interpretations with one survey of 80 different studies finding 43 definitions for the terms traveller, tourist and visitor. Among the various definitions, the most useful and comprehensive definition is given by Cohen and Smith. Cohen describes the tourist as 'a voluntary, temporary traveller, travelling in the expectation of pleasure from the novelty and change experienced on a relatively long and non-recurrent round-trip'. According to Smith, 'ellopsis, etc ... in general, a tourist is a temporarily leisured person who voluntarily visits a place away from home for the purpose of experiencing a change' (1989:1).

International tourism became a major modem mass phenomenon after World War II when it came to embrace practically all social classes in industrialised Western societies. This expansion was made possible by rising standards of living and the shortening of the work year, which were accompanied by longer paid vacations in the industrialised Western countries and a rapid improvement in the means of transportation (Dumazdier 1967:129–30; Young 1973:30). To these factors the enhanced motivation to travel should also be added; it will be discussed below.

In 1996, according to the figures of the World Tourism Organisation (WTO) and the World Travel and Tourism Council (WTTC), there were more than 560 million global travellers generating a total global income of over 3.6 trillion US dollars. There were 255 million employed in this industry, which is 1 in every 9 of the world's total workforce (Kunwar, 1997: 6).

Tourism is temporary movement of people to destinations outside their normal places of work and residence, the activities undertaken during their stay in those destinations and the facilities created to cater to their needs. The study of tourism is the study of people away from their usual habitat, of the establishments which respond to the requirements of travellers and of the impacts that they have on the economic, physical and social well-being of their hosts. It involves the motivations and experiences of the tourists, the expectations of and adjustments made by residents of reception areas and the roles played by the numerous agencies and institutions which intercede between them.

Citing Thiem (1994), Luger (2000) writes, 'The networked cultures model is based on an inter cultural research approach. Its starting point is the interaction between the culture of the sending region (the place the visitors come from, usually cities), the holiday culture (the lifestyle of the tourists as holiday makers), the service culture (the lifestyle of the local people in the receiving region in their function as hosts), and the culture of the destination (the original, traditional culture of the destination)'. There are a number of interfaces between these four different cultures, and the direct contact between tourists and their hosts is at the interface between holiday culture and service culture. This interaction—according to the hypothesis—leads to changes in all four cultures, transports aspects of town life to the rural areas and leads to the creation of new professions in the service culture (Luger, 2000:38).

One of the most important aspects of tourism is product. Scholars conceptualise tourism products as a bundle of activities, services and benefits that constitute the entire tourism experience. The bundle consists of four components: destination attractions, destination facilities, accessibility image and the price (see Smith, 1994:584). Lewis and Chambers (1989:36) consider the tourism product to be composed of goods, environment and services. According to them, the product can be viewed on three different levels: formal product, core product and the augmented product. In the first type, the tourist believes he is buying, in the second, the tourist is actually buying and in the third, though it is core, any other value addition by the supplier. But, according to Smith (1994:586), the tourism product comprises five different elements: physical plant, service, hospitality, freedom of choice and involvement. Overall, there comes wants, needs and structure of the product and satisfaction.

The tourism industry is a complex, multi-layered phenomenon which includes travel agencies, tour operators, airlines, cruise lines, car rental agencies, credit card companies, public relation firms, tourism bureaus and the media. In the host country it includes inbound transport operators, ground transporters, guides, accommodation facilities, natural and pristine parks, other recreational sites, cultural and crafts centers and providers for recreational facilities. The international travel industry is supported by government policies and regulations, infrastructure projects and nowadays, by commercial banks and international institutions (Stephanie, 2001:9).

In addition, tourism has been variously defined (or refined) by governments and academics to relate to such fields as economics, sociology, cultural anthropology and geography. Economists are concerned with tourism's contributions to the economy and the economic development of a destination area, and focus on supply/demand, foreign exchange and balance of payments, employment and other monetary factors. Sociologists and cultural anthropologists study the travel behaviour of individuals and groups of people, and focus on the customs, habits, traditions and life styles of both hosts and guests. The notion of 'life style' can be defined as the specific way of life of a group within society: who does what, when, how, with whom, and why? Geographers are concerned with the spatial aspects of tourism, and study travel flows and locations, development dispersion, land use and changes in the physical environment (Theobald, *op cit.*, 7). Geographers focus mainly on the international, national and regional section of the tourism system; an important concept to understand is the global tourism system with its three constituent parts, the tourist generating region, the transit region and the destination region. These three elements combine with the dynamic human element and the economic element to form the total system (see Gunn, 1976).

REVIEW OF LITERATURE

Finney and Wateson report how tourism research has been looked down upon. Mitchell comments how the study of tourism 'gets no respect' in the discipline of geography. Valene L. Smith reports how her early research interests were actively discouraged. Leiper suggests that as late as 1979 in academe, tourism as a focus of research might well be derided (Crick, 1989:311; Nash, 1996:4). The present researcher felt the similar kind of experience while introducing tourism as a paper in academia.

The history of tourism in Nepal is about 52 years old. The first book on tourism entitled Travel and Tourism in Nepalese Perspectives was written by I.K. Pradhan in 1979. Though tourism was flourishing in Nepal, due to the lack of tourism education, this book could not get academic recognition in the academia. However, the academic credit goes to Mr. Pradhan. After that Yajna Raj Satyal wrote a book on tourism entitled Tourism in Nepal: A Profile in 1988. Though the book has thrown light only on the general aspects of tourism in Nepal, this became at least a source of getting information and knowledge about tourism to the general readers and the students of this discipline. When Tourism was first introduced in 1993 to the students of postgraduate level at the Centre Department of Culture, Tribhuvan University, Satyal's book was prescribed in the syllabus.

Since International Centre for Integrated Mountain Development (ICIMOD) was established, a lot of research works have been carried out by different scholars of economics, geography and other disciplines. The study was confined only in the mountain (Banskota and Sharma, 1995; Sharma, 1995; Shrestha, 1995). These works have contributed a lot for understanding tourism in the context of planning, development, environmental impact and impact of tourism on culture only in the mountain. Prayag Raj Sharma has written a report on Culture and Tourism Defining Roles and Relationship (1995) and has succeeded in analysing the data through the help of some sociological and anthropological theoretical tools developed by leading scholars of sociology of tourism e.g. Erik Cohen. Therefore, Sharma's contribution has become the landmark in the study of cultural tourism, even though the other sociological and anthropological tools applied by Sharma cannot be found. His study is based on macro perspective.

The present researcher got training in tourism at SOAS, London, in 1990. Later on he wrote a book on tourism entitled Tourism and Development Science and Industry Interface in 1997. With a view to providing a wealth of information, ideas, knowledge and theory to the students, researchers, planners and professionals of this academic subject and industry, the author made an effort to write a book based on the structure of tourism. However, this book, except chapter nine was prepared only on the secondary sources. This book introduced the anthropology of tourism for the first time in the history of anthropology and tourism in Nepal.

It is Pitamber Sharma who edited a book entitled Tourism as Development Case Studies from the Himalaya (2000). The central message of the book is simply that tourism, in order to be sustainable in the mountains, has to contribute to the environmental, economic and sociocultural development of tourist areas or else it has no meaning and relevance. But, no doubt, this book has become the main source of knowledge-based platform for understanding mountain tourism.

It is Yajna Raj Satyal who wrote a series of books on tourism in Nepal (2000a, b). These seem to be quite useful to understand the historical development and some statistical data of tourism. He has failed in using the methodological tools and tourism theories.

It is Kamal Maiya Pradhan who has written a book on tourism entitled Planning Tourism in Nepal (1997). Her book is based on the field work of Nagarkot. Her book seems to be relatively quite useful because she has made an effort to apply some theoretical tools in analysing the data. It is Dibya Gurung (1995) who has worked on tourism and gender of Annapurna region. Her work has become another important landmark for the study of gender in the perspective of tourism in Nepal.

Foreign scholars like Adams (1992, 1996), Fisher (1990), Steven (1996), Luger and Inmann (1998), Rogers and Aitchison (1998), Baumgartner (1986) and Luger (2000) have written leading articles and books on tourism related to Nepal. Most of them studied in Khumbu and have developed some concepts. Most of their works are based on the impact of tourism in Khumbu. Adams's 'reconstructed reciprocity' (1992) got world wide recognition in the field of anthropology of tourism. Luger's Kids of Khumbu (Linger, 2000) is another leading book on tourism in which there is shown the heading 'Grandfather Khumbu, Father Kathmandu Son New York—Migration, Education and Mobility'. This gives symbolic meaning of tourism in Khumbu. Fisher has also importantly showed the Sherpa life on front stage and back stage (1990:124). Rogers and Aitchison have shown both positive and negative development of tourism. Luger and Inmann have edited a book entitled Sustainability in Mountain Tourism (1998). There are several papers on mountain tourism written by Price (1995), Kariel (1995), Gurung and Coursey (1994) and Stevens (1997). Their studies are confined only to the Mountainous areas of Mt Everest and Annapurna region. All these papers will be useful for the study of tourism in Nepal. Though tourism has been studied by both the indigenous and foreign scholars, no work has been done on anthropology of tourism in the case of Nepal independently.

The Tharus of Chitwan have been studied by several scholars like Pyakurel (1982), Muller-Boker (1991a, b, c, 1993, 1999), Guneratne (1994, 1996, 1998, 1999) and Mikame (1979). But, no anthropological study of tourism has been carried out in Chitwan except some reports prepared by non- anthropologists. Therefore, realising the importance of anthropological study of tourism, Chitwan-Sauraha, one of the popular tourist destinations, originally inhabited by the Tharus, an indigenous ethnic group of Nepal, has been selected for this study.

While studying tourism in anthropological perspective, the anthropological research methodological tools are applied for the collection of data. Even though few theoretical models of anthropology of tourism has been also applied in this study. The model which has been developed by the above mentioned scholars in the study of Khumbu can not be applied in the study of Sauraha because of the different touristic activities in two different destinations. In this regard, Crick (1989:331) writes, 'Social scientists need to know that rules may be different in different cultures. Different types of tourist may be treated differently, for after all, different types of tourist do affect a culture differently; almost certainly, different classes of people in a culture treat tourists according to different standards. And then there is the 'development cycle' aspect of tourist systems . . . The way tourists are treated today may differ from the way they were perceived and treated 15 years ago.' Finally this is going to be a new contribution in the field of anthropology of tourism.

RESEARCH METHODS APPLIED

As far as anthropological research methodology is concerned, Nunez (1989) has suggested that tourism could be studied under a variety of traditional anthropological rubrics. In analysing contemporary theory, Lett (1987, 1989) has suggested that the paradigms of cultural materialism and symbolic anthropology are best suited for the analysis, respectively, of human life and identity, and he would suggest that holds true as well for the study of tourism. Anthropologists may differ as to whether they wish to study symbolic systems of meaning or behavioral systems of adaptation, but all anthropologists agree that all aspects of sociocultural systems are interrelated and all anthropologists agree that their theories must be applicable to all peoples in all places at all times. The major paradigmatic challenges facing contemporary anthropologists are ones that can readily be pursued in the context of touristic studies, as Greenwood (1989:171–186) notes, when he observes that the 'broadest theoretical issues in the discipline' include 'culture as representation' (the critical issue for symbolic anthropologists) and 'the links between political economy and systems of meaning' (an abiding concern for cultural materialists).

For the first time, the fieldwork was conducted in Sauraha for a short period in March 1993 under a UNESCO project entitled Effects of Tourism on Culture and Environment. Later, the present researcher decided to work on anthropological study of tourism related in Sauraha, one of the most important tourist destination areas of Nepal. Therefore, fieldwork for this study was conducted continuously from 1994 to 2000 always limiting 2–3 weeks. The hoteliers, the naturalists, the grocers, the tourists of different nationalities, the natives and the non-natives were the main sources of information. The data was collected through participant observation group discussions, narrative and biographical interviews, and unstructured interviews. The procedure adopted for this study is based on the fundamental principles of qualitative social research, and the research attempts to find explanations for the social situations and driving forces of the lives of young and old people who are involved in the field of tourism on the one hand and impact of tourism in the destination area on the other.

'Any atempt to study an indigenous population and a tourist population in interaction will probably require talents similar to that of the Roman rider, with a foot on each horse. To make complete, accurate, and empathetic of both populations will neccessitate a delicate balancing act' (Nunez, 1989). Therefore, the researcher has followed participant-observation in both camps (hosts and guests). In order to understand through observation the interactions between hosts and guests one must keep in mind that this interaction, being often instrumental, temporary and distanced, is performed on a stage where stereotypical masks are attributed to others and also worn by one self. Goffman's dramaturgical theory (Goffman, 1959) would support this claim and add that to every staged performance there has been a backstage preparation where hosts and guests have somehow prepared for stage. For example, those who become determinant to visit Nepal, they will have read a guide book to the zone, prepared his wardrobe, sought photographs of the area and its inhabitants or learned a few essential words of Nepali; the host will have learned how to say 'hello' in 5 languages, put on her traditional dress and rehearsed the 'typical Nepali smile'. It is necessary to understand what happens backstage, and not only on stage, to understand the nature of an interaction between hosts and guests.

Following the academic model of Nash (1996), Cohen (1984), Graburn and Moore (1994), Smith (1989) and Butler (1992), the research has been carried out in Sauraha located outside the Chitwan National Park of Nepal. Above all, an anthropologist is a kind of translator, a person with a great depth of knowledge who is a bridge between the inside and outside of a culture, characteristics that can be used to advantage in tourism research (Graburn and Moore, 1994:234).

The question is, how far tourism is responsible for bringing a change in the destination? Is tourism an agent of change? How do the natives perceive the other's culture? If people have undergone changes, what kind of changes are taking place in the destination?

In course of conducting field work in Sauraha, the researcher provided a week's training to the naturalists of Sauraha for improving the cultural briefing on the Tharus of Chitwan with the support of Department of Tourism, Nepal. It is due to that action-oriented anthropological work, that the researcher did not have a problem in collecting the data within the short period of visit at different times in different years. The synchronic study has been supported by diachronic evidences. Both emic and etic approach has been followed in the context of collecting the data. Photography in this kind of study is quintessential. The data is judged through pros and cons method.

Basically, the study's theoretical analysis of tourist interaction is related to Goffman's action-oriented approach. Applying this theory to tourism, one could say that in the 'front stage' world, the interaction between tourists and natives takes place in play acting.

'Back stage' would be the native's daily lives when they get away from the tourists (or in the off-season where there are no tourists around), when they go back to living out their own culture and life rhythm. In some destinations where there are tourists throughout the seasons, the natives will be on the 'front stage' and their culture adds more and more features of service culture.

Another concern of tourist destination is authenticity. Whether the tourists can see the authentic culture or not. In this regard, consider the theory of Boorstin's 'pseudo events', MacCannell's 'staged authenticity' and Turner's 'center out there'.

Similarly, the theory of acculturation or development or tourist as an agent of change has been another concern in this study.

Chapter Two

ANTHROPOLOGY AND ANTHROPOLOGISTS

Anthropology (Moore, 1997:15) addresses a series of questions that humans considered for millennia: What is the nature of society? Why do cultures change? What is the relationship between the person as an individual and the person as a member of a distinctive social group? What are the distinguishing characteristics of humanness? Why are cultures different? Sociology (Donnell, 1992:7) also addresses a series of questions like How is society constructed? How does society operate or function? How are some groups in society more powerful than others? What causes social change? Is society normally in orderly balance or conflict? What is the primary purpose of sociological study?

The answers have been given to these questions by E.B. Tylor, L.H. Morgan, Emile Durkheim and Franz Boas in the field of anthropology and Emile Durkheim, Karl Marx and Max Weber in sociological perspectives (Donnell, *et.al.*, 7-11). In order to explore man and his total cultural system, the anthropologists have proposed a variety of approaches (pure functionalism by Bronislaw Kasper Malinowski; structure functionalism by Alfred Reginald Radcliffe-Brown; Structuralism by Claude Levi-Strauss; ethnolinguistics by A.F.C. Wallace and John Atkin and W. Sturtvant; neo-evolutionism or multilinear evolution, cultural ecology and cultural materialism by Leslie White, Julian Steward and

Marvin Harris; symbolism by Victor Turner, Clifford Geertz and Mary Douglas; feminism and Marxism by Eleanor Burte Leacock; postmodernism by Jacques Derrida, Michael Foucult and Jean-Francois Lyotard).

An important aspect of anthropological research is the field trip. To go into the field and gather data about a particular (often exotic) people at first hand is almost a sacred feature of anthropological culture. The goal of such a trip is to get to know people and to convey that knowledge to others. Most students have to negotiate such a field trip successfully in order to get advanced degrees, and famous names like Franz Boas, Bronislaw Malinowski, Edmund Leach, Clifford Geertz and Margaret Mead are identified with the field study of peoples like the Indians of the northwest coast of America, the Trobrianders, the Kachin, the Balinese or the Samoans. In the field trip, the anthropologist is supposed to live on intimate terms with a particular people—often in difficult circumstances—while getting to know them. This important rite is supposed to involve serious scholarly work. It often does not go easily. Anxiety, rape, accidents, disease and even death are the field worker's lot. The goal of doing serious, scientific work in alien and frequently difficult territory, which eventually produces a picture of a people which does full justice to them and to their way of life, is an assumed—even celebrated—aspect of anthropology. This contrasts with a prevalent view of tourists—all of them travelers, some to far-away, exotic locations—who usually are thought to be bent on enjoying themselves, who rarely gain more than a superficial acquaintance with their hosts and who are very much interested in really understanding them (Nash, 1996:2).

If someone were to ask people on the street what anthropology is all about, they probably would get a number of views. One persistent idea is that anthropologists are concerned with ruins like the pyramids of Teotihuacan outside of Mexico City. Another view is that anthropologists are interested in 'primitives' like the so-called Bushmen of the Kalahari desert in southern Africa or the Walpuri of central Australia, who until recently, still roamed about in a hunting and gathering way of life. Yet another popular notion of the field has anthropologists studying fossils and the evolution of ancient humans such as the Neanderthals of Western Europe (*ibid*, 5).

Like the notions of all those blind men touching the elephant, each of these popular views of anthropology contains an element of truth, but it does not give the whole picture, which involves everything human whenever and wherever it occurs. As far as tourism is concerned, it is the field of sociocultural anthropology, which focuses on peoples' behavior, that is most relevant. Anthropologists have used the term culture to refer to the various activities of human groups or societies. Such activities as tourism do not take place in a vacuum, nor are they unrelated, but rather comprise more or less integrated systems laden with the associative and dissociative tendencies that mark all social life (*ibid*).

Though Franz Boas was concerned with change of human's culture, he never produced any major theory of culture change. But, many students followed Boas's interest in the study of change, they applied their efforts in a more effective way. Where Boas had been concerned with documenting the fact that an innovation had diffused, his followers in the next generation of anthropological investigations became aware of the importance of contact between two or more groups for the diffusion of culture. The result was that between about 1920 and 1950, a major school of anthropology arose, based upon the study of social and cultural change through culture contact, a process known as acculturation. This came out from the study of Mead (1932) on the Plains Indian people, Herskovits (1938) on Caribbean culture and Sharp (1952) on the Yir Yorront tribe of northern Peninsula of Australia. This, later on, gave birth of another new dimension in the field of anthropology, i.e. anthropology of tourism.

As far as the study of tourism is concerned, one of their more important recent concerns has been with culture contact and culture change, particularly where the contact has involved a more powerful, more developed Europe and North America and the less powerful, less developed world of countries such as those in most of Africa or Latin America. The anthropologist Nunez (1977:207–210) has pointed out, the study of Western-inspired acculturation or development among the less developed peoples of the world, as for example, in Wolf's *Europe and the People without History* (1982) or *Worsley's The Three Worlds* (1984), has provided fertile ground for anthropological research on tourism. Indeed, it has continued to dominate such study (*ibid,* 8).

ANTHROPOLOGY OF TOURISM

'Two sides meet in a kind of never-never–land-the empty meeting grounds'.

Dean MacCannell (1992)

'Travellers there are no roads. Roads are made by walking'.

Spanish Proverb (Henry Kissinger, 1994)

Anthropology has important contributions to offer to the study of tourism, especially through a neo-traditional approach that includes the basic ethnography and its national character variant as the acculturation model and the awareness that tourism is only one element in cultural change (Smith, 1980:15).

According to Crick (1989:332), tourism is an odd anthropological object, because international tourists are people out of culture in at least two senses. First they do not belong to the culture of the destination country, and second, they have stepped beyond the bounds of ordinary social reality, into what is sometimes referred to as a 'ludic' or 'liminoid' realm. Wagner expresses the same notion with her phrases 'out of place' and 'out of time'. Since tourism is a highly complex system, countless disciplines, from anthropology and sociology, through recreation geography, social psychology, marketing economics, hotel management studies and so on, all have a view of what goes on (Crick, 1989:312).

According to Nash (1996:90–91), the study of tourism from the anthropological perspective has been carried out from three broad points of view which have provided the basic framework for anthropologists to approach this multifarious subject. First, consider that tourism involves social contact between people from different cultures or sub-cultures. Like migration, it is an intercultural phenomenon, which should appeal especially to anthropological sensibilities. This contact, which involves leisured travellers and those who serve them, takes place in a context that includes at least social groups—home and host—and involves various social transactions between the people involved. Second, the social relationship (in this touristic) has consequences for the individuals and their cultures or sub-cultures. Third, the more or less autonomous groups involved in tourism transactions may be seen to be producing (as well as reproducing) cultures in which tourism plays a part.

Sociologists and anthropologists have studied the dynamics of the tourist system mainly on the regional and local levels. The 'genetic apporach' was pioneered by Forster who drew attention to the processual nature of tourism, which ' "creates a type of cumulative causation, and ultimately a new economic base" (1964:218) as it penetrates a new area. Greenwood's study of Fuenterrabia is the most influential publication in this field (Greenwood, 1972).

Anthropologists tend to take the broad view, examining the historical growth of tourism, tourism in relation to class, life-style and nationality, and in relation to stages of the life-cycle (Graburn and Moore, 1994:234). These authors have discussed anthropology of tourism under the sub-headings of tourism: everyday life, the push factors: a change is as good as a rest, symbolic reversals, attractions and goals; the pull factors: touristic representations between the tourist and the target, anthropological research on the impacts of tourism, social impacts of tourism, ethnicity, unequal relations on large and small scales, ethnic and tourists' arts, interaction between host and guests, alternative tourism, anthropologists as consultants.

For MacCannell, tourism is the quest of modern man; the tourist is a post-industrial man doing ritual obeisance to an elaborate and experientially fragmenting division of labor that requires the search for authenticity in other cultures (Crick, 1989:310).

Regarding the view of MacCannell, Crick (1989:333) writes, 'We should particularly note here the importance of the play concept in post structuralist thinking. It is interesting that our most stimulating and original general discussion of tourism today—MacCannell's (1976) *The Tourist A New Theory of the Leisure Class*—marshals a vast array of approaches; Marxism, semiotics, dramaturgy, and so on, in what is a very modern looking analysis. Yet as Maurice Thurot and Gaetane Thurot claim not only is MacCannell behind the times empirically in terms of the contemporary nature of much international tourism, he is also theoretically out of date. Marxism theory may have been original, but Marx himself retained a somewhat 18th-century concept of human nature in terms of labor and production. We now live in a post-Marxian world of the "political economy of the sign", the emphasis has shifted away from production. We are now interested in what Baudrillard has termed the "mirror of production", and tourism, being so much a matter of leisure, consumption, and image, is an essentially (post)-modern activity'.

Through global integration, those people who previously remained behind their frontiers are now invited to consider themselves part of great multi-cultural units, sometimes alongside former enemies. And tourism, particularly 'cultural tourism' is often considered by international organisations as a pedagogic instrument allowing new identities to emerge—identities corresponding to the new plural-ethnic or plural-state configurations which are forming. It is necessary to distinguish, however, between a desire to construct new identities which is basically motivated by ideology, and those identities which emerge naturally from the working of societies. The task of sociologists and anthropologists is to clarify the second of these (Lanfant, 1995).

With the world wide spread of exchanges our field offers one remarkable thing: the society ordained to be a tourist destination is called upon not only to open its frontiers and its homes to foreign visitors, but also to engage in a very particular trade, which is a question of culture, heritage, traditions and identity itself. Certain parts of the population became merchandised as Meagan Morris, making 'life' itself a 'tourist object' (*ibid*). According to Lanfant et al., 'identity has sense when it is supported by a subject. Identity is the test to which all human beings living in society are constantly subjected. This test is enhanced when the individual is attacked, weakened, marginalised, placed in awkward situations or torn between conflicting interests' (*ibid*).

In the ideal typical sense, basic research in the anthropological study of tourism is aimed at comprehending this field of human action, nothing more. '... tourism is perceived as being within society and the tourists as being an actor in society' (Lanfant et al, 1995). It is Nunez, the first anthropologist, who wrote a paper on anthropology of tourism entitled 'Tourism, Tradition and Acculturation: Weekendismo in a Mexican Village' in 1963 and this was published in *Ethnology*. Since then a lot of anthropologists took interest in the new field. The first anthropological symposium on tourism was held in Mexico City in 1974 and it has been conducted every year since then. This gave birth to a new academic field in both anthropology and tourism. Nunez, in his study, documented the interaction between Mexican villagers and urban tourists, noting rapid and dramatic changes in economic and political structures, land use patterns, and value system. McKean (1976) found similar results in a study undertaken with Taos Pueblo Indians. He describes, they have to be allied in a cultural symbiosis with the Anglo motel and shop operators, recognising the importance of the Indians in attracting tourists and the Indians knowing that the whites operates necessary tourist services that enable them both to profit.

Although applied anthropology enjoys a unique and

well-established position within the discipline, applied anthropologists have only recently turned their attention to problems associated with tourism. Considering the rich potential for research and practice in the field it is surprising that there is so little precendence for this volume (cf. Johnston 1990; Smith, 1992, citedin Chambers, 1997:8).

Cohen dates the first full length sociological study of tourism to the 1960s (Crick, 1989:310). Anthropologists studying tourism have tended to approach tourism as a form of acculturation or development, as a personal transition for the tourist and as a kind of social superstructure (Nash, 1996:16, 84). The anthropology of tourism focuses mainly on cross-cultural relationship, interaction between hosts and guests in terms of the natives—the weaker hosts and the tourists, the stronger guests and socio-cultural impact of tourism in the host society (Smith, 1989). Cohen (1984:383) clearly writes, the impact of tourism is by far the most intensively researched issue within the sociology of tourism. The sociology of tourism is an emergent specialty concerned with the study of touristic motivations, roles, relationships and institutions and of their impact on tourists and on the societies who receive them (Cohen, 1984:373). He has also identified eight main sociological perspectives on tourism: tourism as commercialised hospitality, as democratised travel, as a modern leisure activity, as a modern variety of traditional pilgrimage, as an impression of basic cultural themes, as an acculturative process, as a type of ethnic relations and as a form of neo-colonialism. The first sociological work on tourism was done by Knebel in 1960 (*ibid*).

MacCannell was the first sociologist to anchor the study of tourism in the mainstream of sociological theory, by relating his analysis to the work of Marx, Durkheim, Levi-Strauss and Goffman in an effort to develop an 'ethnography of modernity' (MacCannell 1976:1).

Lanfant (1993) paints a bleak picture in recounting the difficulties of bringing the subject of international tourism into the mainstream of French sociology (Nash, 1996:2). It has often been said that the appeal of identity in traditional societies meets the demand from Western tourists for authenticity. Anthropologists in the field—Danielle Rozenberg, Shelly Shenhav-Keller, Jean Michaud, Michel Picard, Edward Bruner and Anath Ariel de Vidas—talk about those tourists seeking authenticity who choose to visit a place in order to rediscover in themselves an identity which they cannot find in their everyday lives. Ethnic tourists who go to Ladakh or who cross the Andean Cordillera, the hippies who seek another life in Ibiza, Jewish tourists from the Diaspora who go to Maskit, and Australian men who go on sexual trips to South East Asia, all have something in common: an interest in an authentic other place. Should tourism lead to another possible life, a real life where for a time the individual can meet his or her 'true' self (Meyer, 1988, cited in Lanfant, 1995:9)?

Lanfant further expresses, 'On the one hand, the spread of tourism in the world economy leads to extroversion. On the other hand, it works towards the retrenchment of identities in a territory, a system of filiation and patrimony, all acting as a fulcrum. There is a constant tug-of-war between mobility, which is motivated by a zest for modernity, and an appeal to identity, which takes for granted the equality of cultures on their own terms'.

The sociology of international tourism cannot ignore these two sides of the analysis. It must take into account the fact that international tourism, through a series of actions, fits into the process of globalisation, without ignoring the local approaches.

On a scientific level one observes a similar double polarity. While one trend asserts itself within sociology, which places emphasis on the world-wide spread of social phenomena (Archer, 1991, cited in Lanfant, 1995), a new tendency is becoming apparent which boasts the 'indigenisation' of sociology. Celebrating diversity, on behalf of the right to be different, this new tendency thus aspires to better defend cultural specificities and ethnological heritage (Akiwowo, 1988; Park, 1988, cited in Lanfant, 1995).

For some people this double polarity, which asserts itself simultaneously in the field of sociology, seems like an opposition which puts globalisation and indigenisation back to back. There is no need to oppose these two trends, to make rivals of an integral sociology and a differential sociology, a macro-sociology and a micro-sociology, a holistic model and selective studies. Sociology observes the phenomenon of homogenisation, of uniformity, whilst at the same time recording the creativity of the social field. There is no reason to contrast unity and diversity, or to oppose global and local, identity and change. Rather we must fasten on to the tension between these poles in two respects: the global world which encompasses all the individual 'particles' in motion, and lively differentiation governed by universal exigencies. In fact the trickiest problem for the sociologist studying international tourism is to grasp the analysis at both ends and to know how to master it. The sociology of international tourism is a sociology of 'communication and of complexities' (Morin, 1991, cited in Lanfant, 1995). It is not a new anthropology establishing itself in the web of international tourism.

The great bulk of the impact studies focus on the host community or society; the effect on the tourists' country of origin is neglected. Anthropological and sociological analyses of the impacts of tourism have increased rapidly in the past decade (Mathieson and Wall, 1982:159). Many scholars have assumed

(1) that tourism may bring about rapid and dramatic changes in the loci of authority, land-use patterns, value systems and portions of economy;
(2) that tourism is a legitimate and necessary area of cultural change research and
(3) that the study of tourism may proceed to another laboratory situation for the testing of acculturation theory.

Certainly the tourist today is more ubiquitous than the missionary, the technical assistance agent or the trader, all of whom are considered as agents of diffusion and acculturation (Nunez, 1963:152). The impact of tourism on customs and the arts has been extensively drawn into the economic domain or 'commoditised' (Greenwood, 1989) as resources to encourage tourism. The fact that this occurs is commonly accepted but the question of their transformation and debasement through tourism is still hotly debated. 'Commoditisation' does not, in itself, necessarily change customs or the arts. Indeed, in some instances, it may conserve them in the interest of tourism (Aspelin, 1977). In most cases, customs and the arts have, in fact, undergone changes as they have been addressed to a new 'external' Public (Graburn, 1976c:1–32; McKean, 1976b:242–243) that does not share the cultural background, language and values of the traditional 'internal' public; dances and rituals have been shortened or embellished and folk customs or arts altered, faked and occasionally invented for the benefit of tourists. (e.g. Boorstin, 1964:108; Graburn, 1976c:19–20).

Lanfant (1995) while disagreeing tourism as a force of social change coming to destroy territorial and local identities, thinks that local society and tourism as being in relations of exteriority.

In an interesting comparison, Butler (1992:138–139) lays out what he believes to be the general characteristics of three kinds of tourism impact assessment carried out by social scientists: that conducted by academics (who, presumably, are more likely to be practicing basic science), research for private clients and that for clients in the public sphere. He believes that though there are a good many exceptions, these three kinds of investigations tend to differ in a number of ways. Butler (1992:138) points out, for example, that 'private sector studies ... have traditionally been predictive studies, generally concentrating on economic impacts ... and focusing on the benefits of tourism to proponents and communities', while studies done by academics 'for the most part, have been post-development assessments and have often focused upon the negative or undesired effects of tourism and related developments'.

Ritchie's suggestion that academics, in contrast to applied researchers, 'though also concerned with strategic issues of immediate concern, often have an interest in more fundamental or basic research addressing major issues with medium or long-term implications' also seems to ring true for the anthropological study of tourism (Nash, 1996:145).

There were, however, a few early researchers, for example, McKean (1976) in Bali, Cohen (1979a) in Thailand, Boissevain (1978) in Malta and Hermans (1981) on the Costa Brava, who found tourism to be a benign and possibly beneficial agent of change. Others, for example those attending a seminar convened by the World Bank (de Kadt 1979), thought that tourism could have a range of consequences ranging from good to bad, but with proper intervention, benefits could be made to exceed the costs for host people. Greenwood (1989) lamented, 'local culture ... is altered and often destroyed by the treatment of it as a tourist attraction. It is made meaningless to the people who once believed in it'. But in his second analysis of the festival, written as an epilogue, Greenwood questioned whether tourism has any unique effects in transforming culture, as opposed to, say, mass communications and economic globalisation. He concluded, 'Some of what we see as destruction is construction; some is the result of a lack of any other viable options; and some the result of choices that could be made differently' (Getz, 1997:316). Applied research, such as impact assessments by Pye and Lin (1983) for Asia, Preister (1987) for an American ski resort and the World Tourism Organisation for Bhutan (Smith, 1981) have followed in this vein. Proper intervention, however, has turned out to be a highly problematic thing.

To understand tourism, Jafari's model is also equally important. He sees tourism through four major platforms known as advocacy platform (which always subscribes to tourism development and promotion), cautionary platform (which warns against the consequences of tourism), adaptancy platform (which prescribes alternative form of tourism), and knowledge-based platform (which is always in search of a deeper understanding of tourism) (Nash, 1996).

As far as the tourist search is concerned, for Boorstin (1962) it is 'pseudo-events', for MacCannell (1976) it is 'authenticity', and for Turner (1973) it is 'center out there'. An increasingly key factor in the tourist search is nostalgia, which is closely related to authenticity. That nostalgia motivates and attracts tourists can also be taken as evidence of dissatisfaction with modern life and of the search for simpler or more morally uplifting qualities in other places, times or cultures. Nostalgia is now a powerful force not only in North America but especially in Europe (Lowenthal, 1985; Home, 1984, cited in Graburn and Moore, 1994) and Japan (Graburn 1983b). The criticism can be made of the centrality of nostalgia as a motivational force as of authenticity, that is only applies to the more educated, snobbish tourists.

In the word of Crick (1994:81–82) 'whether Turner's remarks are ethnographically accurate is not my concern here. Some Melanesian societies would seem to possess a conceptual distinction like our own. But since the terms 'play' and 'work' are problematic, I will broaden my view from a binary opposition to a triad—a triangle deplacements—constituted by fieldworkers, tourists and pilgrims. Adding the third term will enable further traces between tourism and anthropology to come into focus, because tourists, anthropologists and pilgrims all share displacement into non-ordinary space and time'.

Marxist interpretation of tourism is based on commodity leisured travel. The postmodern concept is based on critical theory. '...one could also argue that

- *(i)* tourism existed in classical (pre-capitalist) Greek and Roman times
- *(ii)* tourism is also a major feature of late Marxist societies,
- *(iii)* it is much less characteristic of there with boring low-paid jobs than of the self-actuating upper-middle classes, and
- *(iv)* not all tourism is so phenomenologically unfulfilling as these authors claim (Graburn and Moore, 1994:235).

Anthropologists have for many years observed that people see the need to have structured breaks from their normal everyday routine of life. In the past these breaks from the normal routine have taken the form of play, ritual, ceremony, worship, festivals, pilgrimage, meditation etc. Initially the majority of research into tourist motivation was designed to determine the 'pull' factors of a destination in motivating people to travel (i.e. the ability of a destination to attract visitors). It is only in the last few years that the 'push' factor (the individual's internal reason for going) has been studied in greater detail and with it has come some surprising discoveries (Krippendorf, 1986:131; Jackson 1989;92–93; Graburn and Moore, 1994).

The push factor for some people is to escape to a new environment. Some group of travellers experience the push factor through a need to escape from a busy and demanding work and home environment. The tourists like honeymoon groups, divorcees, pre or post college 'drifters', retired cruises and major occupational change breaking groups make tour due to their internal reasons. Executives in competitive high pressure jobs, those striving for promotion or those such as doctors and nurses and those in other similar jobs with stressful decision-making and responsibility need breaks to enable both mental and physical renewal. These people seek peace and tranquillity and a change of pace at a holiday destination.

Holidays have become structured breaks in modern industrial societies and individuals in these societies have an expectation of travelling during these holiday periods. In the same way as religious ceremonies or social rituals in earlier societies provided an opportunity to get away from the mundane, so is tourism providing the escape for the citizens of the developed societies.

In this context tourism is seen as a ritual or play. Ritual is characterised by three phases, the first being the separation phase in which participants in the ritual make a conscious recognisable break with the ordinary functions of everyday life. This separation could have been physical separation (e.g. going to church or visiting a sacred site), a visual separation (e.g. painting the body, donning a costume or wearing a mask) or a mental separation (e.g. entering meditation or a trance like state). The second phase was the ritual itself, being a non-ordinary activity such as a festival, church service or a funeral ceremony. Finally the last phase sees an end to the ritual and a return to the ordinary activities of everyday life (Jakson, 1989:96–97).

Traditional religious rituals tended to be performed as social celebrations rather than individual rituals. The modern ritual of tourism tends to be performed away from the home community and as such is more individualistic. Communities also mark weekly, monthly, yearly or seasonal events with ritual ceremony. Examples are harvest festivals, Easter or birthdays. These recurring rituals form the basis of much tourist activity and are known as the 'rites of intensification' (*ibid*).

There are many determining factors in an individual's approach to tourism but they can be placed in three main categories. These are cultural self-confidence, ritual inversions and discretionary income. Cultural self-confidence is determined to a large extent by the family environment and the educational experience. In this category, people become the travellers from upper and middle level socio-economic group. The cultural self-confidence of this group allows them to take the adventurous approach and to discover the world and its sights, history, culture and people. Styles of touristic experiences range from nostalgic through to adventurous. Those seeking a nostalgic experience find satisfaction in confirming the familiar (repeated tour to the same destination) whereas the adventurous traveller seeks excitement and the unexpected.

Ritual inversion can be a motivation affected by both the push and pull factors. The pull factor offers destinations which have characteristics such as the destination of cultural tourism, ethnic tourism, historical tourism, environmental tourism and recreational tourism. Obviously income is a determining factor in people's decision to travel. Income determines the style of holiday chosen by the tourist.

Psychologists have identified the inherent need in people for recognition of existing status and also a need to achieve higher status. If this recognition of status does not come in a work situation, which is often the case, particularly for those in the lower socio-economic groupings, then the status is sought in other activities. As they end their working career they experience a loss of the recognition and status the job brought with it. Other activities are undertaken to gain the needed recognition and can be in the fields of sports, music, arts, clubs and associations or any number of other leisure time pursuits. Travelling serves this purpose very well as it can gain the person recognition and status in many different ways. Before a person travels status can be gained by being able to 'trip drop' in the same way as others 'name drop'. This group can also choose a destination, and standard of accommodation, which will allow them to mix with higher status people than they are able to mix with at home (*ibid*).

The fact that anthropologists have begun to build a sizeable body of literature on the subject of tourism has had several predictable results, including the fact that anthropologists have disagreed about the best theoretical approach to take in examining tourism. The anthropological literature on tourism can be broadly divided into two categories—a division that is reflected in the two articles of Graburn (1989) and Nash (1989). On the one hand, Graburn is interested in exploring the culturally defined meanings that the experience of tourism holds for the tourist and those he or she encounters; on the other hand, Nash is interested in assessing the range of empirical effects that tourism has upon the sociocultural systems of host societies.

Professors Graburn and Nash, in fact, have been actively involved in a debate about the best way to study tourism since 1977. In the past decade, two major theoretical overviews on the anthropology of tourism have appeared, one by Nash (1981) and the other by Graburn (1983a). Graburn has argued that tourism can best be analysed as a near-universal manifestation of the pan-human need for play and recreation whose origin is grounded in the invariable tendency for human beings to assign meaning to their activities, while Nash has argued that tourism can be best viewed as a near-universal form of travel pursued by people at leisure whose origin cannot be determined but whose cultural variability can be assessed. Graburn (1983) suggests that tourism is preeminently a secular ritual, and that in many contemporary societies it fulfills functions once met by sacred (or, more precisely, supernatural) rituals. Nash (1984) questions Graburn's contention that the need to alternate between ordinary and non-ordinary experiences is innate or universal, and he asks why such a need, if it did exist, would necessarily express itself in touristic form. While Graburn would prefer to explore the symbolic meaning of tourism, Nash would prefer to analyse the political and economic effects of touristic development (Nunez and Lett, 1989:276). These two perspectives are not necessarily contradictory.

The theoretical difference between Professors Graburn and Nash is a common one in anthropology, for it reflects the distinction between those who wish to study the maintenance of human identity and those who wish to study the maintenance of human life. These phrases are the same that Lett (1987) has used elsewhere to characterise the basic duality of the anthropological domain of inquiry. By 'the maintenance of human identity', he meant those activities whose primary function is to define and demarcate human status, or those activities whose express origin lies in the human tendency to impose symbol-mediated meanings upon the world. Cross-culturally, the maintenance of human identity is most frequently accomplished through such activities as ritual, play and art. By 'the maintenance of human life', he meant those activities whose primary function is to satisfy the physical and metabolical requirements of survival. Cross-culturally, the maintenance of human life is invariably accomplished, except in the most extraordinary circumstances, through learned and shared subsistence strategies. While most cultural phenomena simultaneously involve, in some aspect, the maintenance of both human life and human identity (this is certainly true of tourism), most anthropologists tend to focus on one set of issues or the other when researching any cultural phenomenon (and this, again, has been true of the anthropological approach to tourism). Thus in analysing tourism most anthropologists have either described the ways in which tourism is used as a symbolic means of expressing and maintaining human identity, or they have described the social, political, economic and environmental effects that result from using touristic modes of production to maintain human life.

While citing the debate of Graburn and Nash, Pearce puts it, 'we need detailed empirical work on tourist behaviors and motivation, not ideological and committed debates about the meaning of tourism. Play itself is a difficult theoretical notion, ...' The anthropology of play is still an undeveloped field.

TOURIST TYPOLOGY

Tourist typologies can be grouped into two general categories:

(i) interactional type and
(ii) cognitive–normative models, which stress the motivations behind travel.

Cohen (1972) first developed four types of tourists, namely, Drifter, Explorer, Individual mass tourist and Organized mass tourist. All the four types are categorised under the theme of interactional model. They are further divided into non institutionalised traveller (drifter and explorer) and institutionalised traveller (individual mass and organised mass). The drifter tourists are always in search of exotic and strange environment.

On the basis of these two dimensions, a fourfold typology of drifters can be constructed:

I. Full-Time Drifters

(1) *Outward oriented:* The 'Adventurer', the original individual drifter, as described in my earlier paper.
(2) *Inward oriented:* The 'Itinerant Hippie', the travelling drop-out, on his way to some drug-sanctuary in Europe or Asia or drifting aimlessly from one 'hippie' Community to another.

II. Part-Time Drifters

(3) *Outward oriented:* The 'Mass-Drifter', usually the college

youth, who spends a limited amount of time to see the world, meet people and 'have experiences', but tends to stick to the drifter tourist establishment of cheap lodgings and eating place and cut-rate fares.

(4) Inward oriented: The 'Fellow-Traveler', the youth who associates with the 'hippies' or other drop-outs, and models his behaviour on these roles, but remains marginal to the 'hippie' sub-culture. He frequents the pop discotheques and boutiques, dresses 'in style', visits the 'hippie' communities for short periods of time, but after his trip he returns to his ordinary pursuits. He is a 'part-time drop out', and parallels the 'week-end hippie' discussed by Yoblonsky.

The original drifter would move among the people and live with them; these were often ordinary folks, as yet removed from the commercialism and incipient modernism of the more sophisticated sectors of the host society. They would receive the drifter as a guest in a traditional manner and he would accept their hospitality.

The political leadership and the local authorities in many countries became increasingly more hostile: drifters were represented as a nuisance, exasperating the locals by strange and immoral behavior; a source of contamination for the local youth; and a general threat of 'cultural pollution'. They were viewed in the image of the longhaired hippie. Their search for drugs, and particularly their use of some non-European countries, in which drugs are permitted as drug-sanctuaries, was resented.

The explorer tourists arrange their own trip and try to get off the beaten track. The individual mass tourists arrangements are made through a travel agency to popular destinations. Organised mass tourists search for familiar travel in the security of own environmental bubble and guided tour.

Like Cohen, Smith (1989:11–13) has also identified seven types of tourists:

(i) Explorer: They are very limited in number, looking for discovery of new places and involvement with local people. They easily accommodate with local people.

(ii) Elite: These are special individually tailored visitors to exotic hammocks, get thoroughly bitten by chiggers, eat native food and chance the tourist 'trots'.

(iii) Off-bat: They desire to get away from the crowds or heighten the excitement of their vacation by doing something beyond the norm. These tourists include those who currently visit Toraja Regency to see the funerals, 'trek' in Nepal to go alone to Point Hope as part of an Alaskan tour.

(iv) Unusual: They visit with peculiar objectives such as physical danger or isolation. These groups tend to be 'interested in the primitive' culture but are much happier with the 'safe' box lunch and bottled soda rather than a native feast. These tourists of both approaches indicate the strong links between visitor expectations–motivations and the structure of destination areas.

(v) Incipient Mass: A steady flow traveling alone or in small organised groups using some shared services.

(vii) Mass: The general packaged tour market leading to tourist enclaves in overseas. This type of tourism is built upon middle-class income and values, and the impact of sheer numbers is high. There is a continuous influx of visitors who inundate Hawaii most of the year, and other areas at least seasonally, including European resorts, and Northern Hemisphere 'winter vacation' land such as coastal Mexico and the Caribbean.

(viii) Charter: Mass travel to relaxation destinations which incorporate as many standardised western facilities as possible. These tourists arrive on mass, as in Waikiki, and for every 747 planeload, there is a fleet of at least 10 big buses waiting to transfer them from the airport to the designated hotel, in the lobby of which is a special Tour Desk to provide itineraries card and other group services.

Among the interaction models of Cohen (1972) and Smith (1989), Cohen classifies tourists according to the degree with which they seek familiar or strange settings and whether or not they are willing to be institutionalised (organised) in their travel. Smith presents a more detailed breakdown incorporating recent market development such as the unorganised hippie treks to Nepal and the social implications of a highly structured charter business. As mentioned above a cognitive–normal typology suggested by Cohen (1979) seeks to distinguish visits in terms of what they mean for the traveller. The typology he gives is best on personal experience:

(*i*) Recreational and
(*ii*) Diversionary (under the theme of search for pleasure),
(*iii*) Experiential,
(*iv*) Experimental and
(*v*) Existential (under the theme of modern pilgrimage).

As far as first one is concerned, this is one of the commonest forms of tourism where the trip is designed to relieve the strains and tensions of work with no deeper significance involved. The second type of visit is a pure escape from the boredom and routine of home life. Accordingly, the third type of tourist seems to be the modern pilgrim looking for authenticity in the lives of other societies because he has seemingly lost his own. In the fourth category, the traveller is in search of alternative lifestyle and is to engage in authentic life of others. The nature of the fifth category is to leave the world of everyday life and practicality to escape to elective center for spiritual sustenance. Visit to South America on an organised tour and buying an optional 1-day package tour to visit the Kuna Indians is an alternate to a day of shopping in duty free Panama.

Studying this topological phenomena, Kumar (1995) comments that the typology suggested by Cohen is based on unique philosophical manner. As he writes, 'One will hesitate to accept his scheme at least the two last types (Experimental and Existential), which appear philosophical rather than realistic. To a large extent, the first three are realistic in nature. However, this typology is incomplete in nature. He further writes, many of the new types have originated not in advanced countries, but in developing countries (particularly different activities of sea beaches). From the geographical basis, there can be incoming, outgoing and internal tourists. Some tourists who are always on the move with a short span of stay are called the tourists belonging to Roving tourism. On the basis of purpose of visit the tourism can be holiday tourism, business tourism, religious; social, business sporting, sporting, recreational, leisure of human kind (*ibid*, 20). The footnote no. 27 of Kumar's article shows that he did not see the original article of Cohen. Therefore, the author seems to be confused whether he is talking about the tourist typology or tourism typology. In the above typology, Smith has widely covered many facts of modern tourism. She has thrown light on the free inclusive tours, group inclusive tours, charter tours, allocentricism and adventurous types of tourism. But she has overlooked the traditional types of tourists. As a whole, this typology is not enough to cover all types of tourists (*ibid*, 1995:19).

Psychographic research applied to the tourism industry has identified two diametrically opposite groups: the allocentric traveler and the psychocentric traveler. Plog (1972) who carried out much of this research, theorises that the population is composed of people with characteristics on a continuum from allocentric to psychocentric of each psychographic market segment and understands how the built-environment corresponds to these characteristics. Plog's major work has been shown by Reime and Cameron (1980). According to these authors, Plog's work emphasises that in choosing a destination, the allocentric seeks a culture and environment markedly different from his own. Research has shown that allocentrics as a group have proportionately higher income than most individuals. As such, the allocentric usually flies to destinations 'off the beaten path'.

The allocentric discovers new destinations by word of mouth from other allocentrics or by assimilating information from diverse and usually technical sources. The allocentric group does not constitute a significant or profitable market segment. Although an allocentric will devote considerable time and money to discretionary travel, the majority of his expenditures are for transportation to and from the destination.

The above-mentioned authors opine that the near-allocentric represents the first market segment capable of being attracted to a planned tourism development. The near-allocentric region will have a culture and a climate different from those of the visitor's home.

The built-environment in near-allocentric destinations should contain accommodation and food-service facilities of excellent quality. While the physical design of these facilities should reflect the historical or cultural style of the region, the standards of quality, comfort and service must always be on a world-class level. The allocentric and the near-allocentric tourists are always seeking new intellectual and recreational experiences.

Mid-centrics are far more conservative than their allocentric and near-allocentric contemporaries. They have a high need for security and peer approval and will not visit any new destination until it is fully accepted by the near-allocentric market. A mid-centric tourist selects a destination with a markedly different climate and some minor cultural differences, but in all other aspects quite similar to his own. As a group, they prefer a well-developed tourism plant with a wide range of commercial attractions.

Walt Disney World is often used to further the argument that mid-centric destinations can be developed 'from scratch'. Theme parks, in general, appeal to the mid-centric tourist by providing a wide variety of experiences without any threat of cultural shock.

The more realistic example of mid-centric tourism destinations would be resorts in the Caribbean, the Bahamas or Hawaii. These regions appeal to mid-centrics because of climate and the fact that the tourists can observe different cultures from a somewhat elevated vantage point.

The true psychocentric tourists prefer a totally familiar environment at the destination and seek commonplace activities such as sunbathing or amusement parks. They expend virtually all their time and resources within the tourism plant; they therefore require a high density built-environment, including modern chain type hotels, family restaurants, tourist/souvenir shops and commercial tourist attraction.

TOURISM TYPOLOGY

Regarding tourism typology, Smith (1989:4–5) distinguishes five forms of tourism defined on the basis of different kinds of leisure mobility undertaken by the tourist and identified as

(i) ethnic tourism
(ii) cultural tourism,
(iii) historical tourism,
(iv) environmental tourism and
(v) recreational tourism.

Ethnic tourism is marketed to the public in terms of the 'quaint' customs of indigenous communities like Eskimos, the San Blas Indians of Panama and the Toraja in Indonesia. Destination activities are characterised by visiting native homes and villages for observation of fabrics and ceremonies, and shopping for primitive wares or curios. As long as the flow of visitors is sporadic and small, host–guest impact is minimal.

As far as Cultural Tourism is concerned, this includes the 'picturesque' or 'local color', a vestige of a vanishing lifestyle that lies within human memory with its 'old style' houses, home-spun fabrics, ox-drawn carts and plows, and handicrafts. Destination activities are also characterised by taking meals in rustic inns, folklore performances and costumed wine festivals. This is peasant culture, illustrated by the case studies on Bali and Spain. Host–guest stresses may be maximal because the rural peasant areas are often readily accessible from tourists resorts, and large numbers of visitors come for the very purpose of observing and photographing the lives of peasants who become objects of study.

In the historical type of tourism, people generally visit museums and cathedrals for the purpose of knowing the glories of the past, i.e., Rome, Egypt and Inca. Favored destination activities include guided tours of monuments and ruins. Host–guest contacts are often impersonal and detected.

Environmental tourism is often ancillary to ethnic

tourism, attracting a tourist elite to remote areas such as Antarctica to experience a truly alien scene. This type of tourism is primarily geographic, many education-oriented travellers enjoy through mountains and country side to observe man–land relationships. Recreational tourism is often sand, sea and sex—promoted by beautiful colour pictures that make you want to be 'there'—on the ski slopes, the palm-fringed beaches, the championship golf course or sunning in a deck chair that attracts tourists who want to relax or commune with native. Destination activities are mostly confined to the sports, curative spas or sunbathing. They might have good food and convivial entertainment. There is a good example of Las Vegas where the guests visit for gambling, 'name' shows and the way-from-home freedom to indulge in the new morality. The typology of tourism—ethnic, environmental, cultural, historical, recreational—presented by Smith (1989) is valid in mountain areas like elsewhere. However, three additional types should also be recognised in these areas. Historically more important than at present, but still of great significance at many resorts in the mountains of Europe and the USSR, is health tourism, relying on both climate and mineral springs. A second type is business/congress tourism, which is an increasingly important component, especially in the Alps and the Rocky Mountains, where it allows resorts developed mainly for skiing to attract customers in the off-season. A third, novel type, which may be termed 'garbage tourism', occurs in both the Andes and the Himalayan (Richter, 1989). The rapid growth of trekking and mountaineering in these regions led to the accumulation of large amounts of garbage along trails and at campsites. Tourists, primarily from North America, now visit these areas specifically to remove this accumulation. There have even been expeditions to the Everest and K2, the world's highest mountains for the same purpose. It is perhaps worth noting that Nepalese Sherpas, at least, do not necessarily regard such 'pollution' as a problem (Fisher, 1990).

Each touristic type has its own special scale of values and its hierarchy of prestigious places, i.e. those having more magic. However, two or more kinds are frequently combined in one trip. For instance, one might visit the museums and cathedrals in Europe (historical) then go to Northern Scandinavia to see the midnight sun (environmental) and the Lapps (ethnic) or one might combine the historical, cultural and ethnic trips by touring in India (Graburn, 1989:32).

Smith's typology is based on a combination of the number of tourists and their adaptation to local norms, while Cohen's typology of tourists roles (Cohen, 1972) is based on the extent of the tourist's exposure to the strangeness of the host environment as against his seclusion within the 'environmental bubble' of his home environment that is supplied by the touristic establishment.

TOURISTIC 'TRADITIONS'

In tourism studies, if the touristic theoretical 'traditions' are missed by the students of this subject it remains always incomplete. Therefore, realising the importance of these theoretical 'traditions' developed by different scholars like D.J. Boorstin, D. MacCannell and Victor Turner who have come from three different backgrounds—history, sociology and anthropology respectively—has been shortly depicted from Cohen (1988:30–41). Boorstin's theory is known as 'pseudo-events'; MacCannell's 'authenticity' and Turner's 'center out there'.

Pseudo-Events

Boorstin's principal intellectual concern is with the contrived and illusory nature of the human experience in contemporary American society, with the 'thicket of unreality which stands between us and the facts of life' (Boorstin, 1964:3). His principal argument is that contemporary Americans do not experience 'reality', but thrive on 'pseudo-events'. The modem mass tourist serves as a prime illustration of his argument. Boorstin's chief claim in his essay on 'the lost art of travel' is that the modern tourist (in contrast to the traveller of yore) is just a passive onlooker who seeks to enjoy the extravagantly strange from the security of the familiar (Boorstin, 1964:77–117). Isolated from the host environment and the local people, he travels in guided groups and thrives on contrived 'attractions', gullibly enjoying the 'pseudo-events', while blithely disregarding the 'real' world around him.

Boorstin's was the first in a long line of socio-critical publications on tourism both in America and Europe. Nevertheless, Boorstin's brief essay served as an important point of departure for more disciplined writings in the sociology of tourism. Indeed, it could be argued that it provoked the serious sociological study of tourism in the English-speaking world. Boorstin (1964:94–99) argued that the tourist seeks to observe the strangeness of the host environment from the security of his immediate surroundings, such as American-type hotels. The typology helps to qualify Boorstin's general argument that all modern tourists seek illusory 'pseudo-events'.

The further development of Boorstin's basic idea involves a change of perspective. Boorstin's approach was essentially 'diachronic'. He proposed a model for a historical transition 'from Traveler to Tourist'. This was transformed by Cohen (1972) into a synchronic typology of contemporary tourists, one pole of which, the 'drifter', corresponded to Boorstin's (historical) traveller, while the other, the 'organised mass tourist', corresponded to his description of the (contemporary) tourist. Such a typology was intended not only to qualify the widely disseminated stereotype of 'the tourist', but also to create the basis for a comparative study of tourism. Her typology is in a sense a further refinement of Cohen's (1972) and thus continues the line of analysis initiated with the criticism of Boorstin's ideas.

Authenticity

MacCannell looks for the ways in which modern man seeks to overcome his predicament, and here his interest turns to the tourist. The image of the tourist which emerges from his work contrasts sharply with Boorstin's. Indeed, it is almost a studied reversal of it. For Boorstin, the tourist expresses the inauthenticity and modernity; for MacCannell he embodies the quest for authenticity. In MacCannell's view (MacCannell, 1973:589–590; 1976, 92–107) indeed, this quest represents the modem version of a universal human concern with the sacred. The tourist is seen as the pilgrim of the contemporary secular world (*ibid*, 1973:593), paying homage to 'attractions,' the symbols of modernity, just as the traditional religious pilgrim paid homage to sacred center.

Moreover, modernity, in MacCannell's view (MaCannell, 1976:8) greedily incorporates the 'pre-modern and 'museumizes' it to be displayed for viewing by modern man so that the touristic 'attractions' are a heterogeneous mix ranging from modern phenomena, such as various 'work-displays' (*ibid*, 1976: 62).

MacCannell's tourist, however, is concerned with the authenticity of the attractions. The quest for authenticity, indeed, rather than the search for contrived illusions, is said to be the fundamental motivation of modern tourists. Since modern man, however, is alienated from his own inauthentic and shallow world, he seeks authenticity elsewhere in other times and other places (*ibid*, 1976:3).

MacCannell's work had a more significant impact on the sociological study of tourism than that of any other researcher before him. An indication of his influence is the fact that it was cited 50 times in the articles appearing in Annals of Tourism Research, in the same 10-year period of 1977–1986, as well as in most other sociological publications on tourism during that period. Moreover, the reaction to MacCannell's approach was less critical than to that of Boorstin. Indeed, many authors have found that MacCannell's concepts—and particularly his twin ideas of 'staged authenticity' and 'tourist space'—helped to illuminate some of their specific research findings.

MacCannell's, like Boorstin's, characterisation of the tourist was too global to be realistic. Hence, it had to be qualified. Just as 'strangeness and familiarity' provided a useful point of departure from Boorstin's paradigm of the tourist to develop a typology of tourist roles, so the concept of 'authenticity' in MacCannell's work provided this author with a starting point for a typology of tourist experiences. A systematic elaboration of this idea (Cohen, 1979a) departed from MacCannell's claim that modern man, in his alienation from his own environment, seeks authenticity elsewhere and so, in fact, becomes a tourist. Assuming, however, that not all moderns are equally alienated, one can hypothesise that they also will not seek authenticity with equal intensity. Rather, these two variables will be directly related: the greater the alienation, the more intensive the quest for authenticity. A fivefold typology of 'modes of (desired) touristic experiences' was therefore developed on the basis of this hypothesis. In order to relate MacCannell's approach to a broader theoretical framework in the study of religion, and expand the typology even further, MacCannell's approach was rephrased in terms of a pair of concepts not utilised by him, but was germane to his general perspective: the concepts of 'the center'(Eliade, 1971:12–17) and of its opposite, 'the other'.

Indeed, he will come closest to the prototypical pilgrim (Turner, 1973:214). This type, however, goes beyond MacCannell's conception of the tourist. His tourist merely seeks a vicarious experience of the authentic life of others, without, however, embracing their life as his own 'elective Center'. With all his alienation, MacCannell's tourist does not strive to abandon modernity. He is the experiential tourist par excellence, an observer, who, though concerned about the authenticity of the other, which he experiences, does not identify with it.

Another of MacCannell's ideas which was taken up and further developed by others is that of 'tourist space'. MacCannell's general concept was developed in Cohen (1979b:26–27) into a fourfold typology based on the distinction between covert and overt tourist spaces on the one hand, and the tourist's impression of whether or not he faces staged tourist space, on the other.

Greenwood (1982:27), without referring expressly to MacCannell, has shown that authenticity 'is a dynamic, emergent phenomenon rather than a static one-and, hence, today's "staged" attractions may turn into "authentic" ones tomorrow. "Authenticity" is thus shown not to be a given, unchanging quality, as implicit in the usage of MacCannell but rather a "negotiable" quality of objects or attractions. From here, it is but a short step to the transition from an "etic" view of authenticity that is, one involving "the interpreter's conceptual apparatus", to an "emic" one, that is, one involving "the adoption of the subjects" viewpoint by the (researcher).'

MacCannell is correct that tourism is a ritual paid to the progressive differentiation of modernity. This paper notes ample illustration of sight-seeing as obeisance to sites which represent modern myths. MacCannell also asserts that tourism is an attempt to grasp the whole of modern life. But the search for the totality is never complete with just one trip.

Center Out There

Of the three theoreticians under review, Turner is exceptional in that he himself did not make any direct contribution to the study of tourism. However, his work on pilgrims (Turner, 1973; Turner and Turner, 1978) and his 'processual' approach in anthropology, and particularly his ideas about liminality, anti-structure (Turner, 1974) and eventually, 'world reversals' (Turner, 1978), have provided an important point of departure for some of the more recent works in the sociology of tourism. In a concise and somewhat simplified manner, Turner's approach can be summarised as follows: People in ordinary, profane life live in social, economic and political structures. In ritual, and particularly the rites-de-passage originally described by Gennep (1960, original edition 1908), the individual is turned out of this structural context. He typically goes through the following three-stage ritual process: first is Separation, both spatial and social. The individual is taken to an unfamiliar place, peripheral to his ordinary place of abode, and separated from his ordinary social group. Second is Liminality: through the separation, the individual has crossed the threshold *(Latin: limen)* of his ordered world, and finds himself in a state of 'anti-structure', 'out of time and place', where his ordinary role and status obligations are suspended and where general human (rather than particular social) bonds are emphasised. He experiences 'communitas', an intensive and undifferentiated bond with the group undergoing the ritual. In this liminal stage, he is confronted with the fundamental symbols of his culture and undergoes a 'direct experience of the sacred, invisible, supernatural order' (Turner, 1973:214). Third is Reintegration: The individual is reintegrated into his ordinary social group usually in new roles and at a higher social status.

Turner's processual model and especially his paradigm of the pilgrimage were attractive to students of tourism, who, from the late 1970s onward, began to adopt it to the study of touristic phenomena. His approach opens completely new and unsuspected perspectives and interpretative possibilities on touristic phenomena. The tourist, like the pilgrim, also moves from a Familiar place to a Far place and returns to the Familiar place (Turner, 1973:213). The tourist's respectful visits to attractions at the Far place, resemble the pilgrim's ascent to the 'Center Out There'.

Boorstin can hardly be said to have founded a 'tradition'. His impact consists mainly in that he formulated a challenging thesis which was then mostly criticised by sociologists. Turner, though not directly engaged in the study of tourism, created a 'tradition' in the fullest sense of the term, with several important empirical studies, conducted mostly with anthropological research methods, adopting an expressly Turnerian theoretical approach. Thus, in principle, he opened the field to analysis from an unbiased sociological and anthropological perspective, although his own perspective did not necessarily fully live up to this ideal.

Boorstin's and MacCannell's approaches are essentially etic. Their approaches are in terms of the following: Image of the Tourist: While Boorstin's image is expressly negative and MacCannell's is implicitly positive, the image of the tourist in the Turnerian 'tradition' is on the whole neutral.

Boorstin's approach focuses on the individual; MacCannell's, at least nominally, on the social structure (though he also relates to the tourist as an individual); and Turner's on the social process, integrating the analysis of individual experience with social dynamics. Level of Analysis: Boorstin's analysis relates primarily to the superficial psychological motives behind the modern touristic experience; MacCannell's to the structural, semiotic significance of tourist setting; while Turner's and his follower's to the deeper, cultural symbolic meaning of the touristic experience within the broader social process.

Direction of the Touristic Quest: All three traditions refer, at least implicitly, to the Center-Other continuum, albeit in different senses, and with contrasting intentions. Boorstin can be interpreted as arguing that modern tourists seek recreation in the Other, but do not engage upon a serious quest for a center.

TOURISM AS AN INDUSTRY OR SOCIAL PHENOMENA

The idea of tourism as a single industry has always remained a debatable issue. Gilpin (1973:107) defines an industry as comprising of all those activities which are directed towards the production of a given class of goods. According to Gilbert (1990:5), 'Industries are made up of firms which produce the same products or groups of products so that the consumer regards these as ideal substitutes for one another even though the products may differ slightly'. Young (1973) describes tourism as a heterogeneous group embracing a large variety of trades and industries that have the supplying of traveller's need as a common function.

Among those supporting the case of tourism being an industry are Wahab (1971), McIntosh (1977), Leiper (1979), Gilbert (1990) and Sinclair (1998). Wahab (1971) deems tourism as an industry whose products are consumed on the spot forming invisible exports. Gilbert (1990:60) considers tourism as an industry in spite of its limitations of not clear boundary delineation or concise conceptual classification. He states that, 'the overall size and impact of spatial and temporal movements of people with varying service needs for shelter, sustenance, entertainment and travel produce basis of an industry'.

Sinclair (1998) views tourism as a collection of interrelated industries and markets. Leiper (1979) deems tourism as an industry consisting of firms, organisations and facilities, which cater to the specific needs of the tourists. According to him, a marketing and design orientation of the individual units forming the industry manifest such an intention of the firms. Leiper describes the industry by dividing it into six functional sectors with each specialising in different kind of service to the tourists. These six sectors are marketing, carriers, accommodation, attractions, miscellaneous services, and regulation.

Regarding industry, economics defines an industry as being a group of independent firms all turning out the same product. Whether or not two products are 'the same' is defined in terms of their substitutability expressed as the cross-elasticity of demand. In lay terms, the more that the purchase of Product A replaces (can be substituted for) the purchase of Product B, the more A and B are the same and hence in the same industry. The second source for definitions is the Standard Industrial Classification (SIC) manuals. Such publications suggest that the SIC system was developed to classify establishments by the type of activity in which they are engaged. To be recognised as an industry, a group of establishments must share a common primary activity and be statistically significant in size. It is clear that the focus of 'industry' is

1. Individual business establishments grouped together.
2. The revenue received by these economic units.
3. Producing and selling a common product, i.e., the product of one firm is a substitute for the product of any other firm in the same industry.

And it is equally clear that the 'manufacturing' sector provides the framework for this focus. Thus, to the extent that tourism is an industry, economists and others will position tourism in terms of these factors: individual businesses, revenues of those businesses and a common product (Davidson, 1997:22).

Jefferson and Lickorish (1988) and Gunn (1994) do not consider tourism as an industry. Jefferson and Lickorish (1988) suggest that tourism cannot be properly described as an industry because it does not produce a single product. Gunn (1994) also does not consider tourism as an industry. He justifies his stand on three arguments. First, the sector does not produce a single product like automobile. Second, the tourism product forming visitors experiences occur at destinations and do not follow the normal industrial product pattern of distribution and transportation to the consumers. Finally, the tourism product is far more perishable than the industrial product, and by nature the product is more of socio-cultural scope than the industrial one.

While rejecting tourism as an industry, Davidson (1997:24) views tourism as

- A social phenomenon, not a production activity.
- The sum of the expenditure of all travellers or visitors for all purposes, not the receipt of a select group of similar establishments.
- An experience or process, not a product, an extremely varied experience at that.

Historically, tourism has not been taken seriously by the economists, economic developers and even government. At best, it is a collection of industries (*ibid,* 20). Tourism is more than an industry. Tourism is more like a 'sector' that impacts a wide range of industries. Tourism is not business or governments—it is people (Davidson, 1994:26).

Tourism has already been recognised by World Tourism Organization (WTO) as 'first world industry', 'a driving force of global development'. From the view point of development in the third world, if there is no other alternative the last choice is tourism (Lanfant, 1995; Crick, 1989:310). Development is the most slippery concept ...and is commonly used in many different ways as well as having changed in meaning over time. John Friedmann has identified at least five dimensions:

1. To suggest an evolutionary process of a positive kind such as rising incomes.
2. In association with words like under, over, or balanced, suggesting it has a structure.
3. As the development of something like a society, a nation or skill.
4. As a process of change.
5. As the rate of change at which the processes occur over time (Lea, 1988:4).

THEORIES OF TOURISM DEVELOPMENT

Efforts have been made to propound the theories of tourism development from time to time by various authors. The theories of tourism development are classified into three broad categories, namely, diffusionist theories, dependency theories, and the formal and informal sector analysis. There are two main theories in diffusionist paradigm. These are development stage theory and the diffusion theory (Browett, 1997). Based on a Euro-American point of view, it inplies that the less developed countries are in an 'earlier phase' of the development process, but will eventually repeat the Euro-American development exprience (Browett, 1982). Schlenke and Stewig suggest that the participation of the population in domestic tourism is closely related to the industrial development of the whole country (cited in Modi, 2001:54). In the process of economic development, the number of social classes that participate in domestic tourism progressively increases.

The main concept underlying the theory is that the development of tourism follows a unilinear path. It implies that the developing countries will be in the same stage after sometime in which the developed countries are today. The basis of this theory lie in Rostow's four stages of economic growth. The four stages according to Rostow are the traditional society, the preconditions to take off, drive to maturity, and the age of high mass consumption.

Applying the Rostow's model to tourism, it is suggested that participation of local population in tourism is closely related to the level of industrial development of the economy. In the stage of traditional society, only the

Theoretical Overview

Economic Stage	*Some Characteristics*	*Examples*
Traditional society	The Underdeveloped World	Much of Africa, Parts of Southern Asia
Long-established, landowning aristocracy, traditional customs, majority employed in agriculture. Very low output per capita, impossible to improve without changing system. Poor health levels, high poverty levels	Economic and Social conditions deny most forms of tourism except perhaps domestic VFR	
Pre-conditions for take-off	The developing world	
Innovation of ideas from outside the system. Leaders recognize the desirability of change	From the take-off stage, economic and social conditions allow increasing amounts of domestic tourism (mainly visiting friends	South and central America; parts of the Middle East, Asia and Africa
Take-off		

Leaders in favor of change gain power and later production methods and economic structure. Manufacturing and services expand	and relatives). International tourism is also possible in the drive to maturity. Inbound tourism is often encouraged as a foreign exchange earner	
Drive to maturity Industrialization continues in all economic sectors with a switch from heavy manufacturing to sophisticated and diversified products		Mexico; parts of South America, Taiwan, South Korea
High mass consumption Economy now at full potential, producing large number of consumer goods and services, New emphasis on satisfying cultural needs	The Developed world Major generators of international and domestic tourism	North America; Western Europe, Japan; Australia; New Zealand

Source: Boniface and Cooper (1987)

country's elite has enough spare time and finances to afford leisure travel. In the process of economic development, the classes participating in tourism increase with the highest level being at the stage of high mass consumption when all sections of the society participate in tourism activities. It is often argued that the development of tourism starts with a pioneer resort and multiplication of resorts leads to a hierarchy and a functional specialisation of resorts (Batta, 2000:42).

The main idea of the diffusion theory is that at one point of the development process, there will be a spread, a filtering, or a diffusion of growth/development impulses from the most developed to the less developed area (Browett, 1982:67). This 'spread', 'trickle down' or 'filtering' effect will lead eventually to an adjustment of the regional disparities after initial polarisation was observed by Alonso (1968). The diffusion theory relies on the assumption that there is a spread or filtering effect from most developed to less developed areas. This theory has been developed on Hirschmann's hypothesis of balanced development (Hirschmann, 1958). It is argued that in order to eradicate backwardness, growth poles are required to be developed. These growth poles can be some regions or particular sectors within the regions having a high multiplier effect. Christaller (1964) was the first to identify tourism to be such a growth center.

The theorists show that tourism gives the economically underdeveloped regions a chance to develop themselves, for these very regions interest the tourists. Tourism was not only considered to have a positive influence on the economy, but it was seen as an 'instrument' in the development of peripheral regions. Because tourism consumption occurs at the place of production, it has, through its numerous associations with other industries (i.e. agriculture, fishery, forestry, building, handicraft), potential multiplier effects on the local economy. However, the multiplier effects have rarely reached the prognosticated level (Bryden, 1973), because a considerable percentage of the spending in periphral regions is drawn away in two ways, namely on a national level toward overseas and on a regional level toward the metropolises (Modi, 2001:55).

The dependency theory arose out of dissatisfaction with the diffusionist paradigm. It maintains that 'as a result of dependency, capitalist development in the core continuously creates and perpetuates underdevelopment in the periphery'. It found its way into tourism studies (Britton, 1982:331–358). The central point or critique of tourism as a development agent was that most development plans and goals were not fulfilled. The multiplier effect were considerably lower than expected owing to high import areas. The paradox arises, therefore, where tourism is being used as a tool for the development of the periphery, but the entire organisation and control resides in the core region. This provides an example of 'organizing the dependence on the core' in order to foster development of the periphery (Husbands, 1981:68).

Khan (1997) analyses the impacts of mass tourism based on dependence theory. He argues that while modern theorists might look at the mass tourism development in the third world as beneficial to the economy with its employment, income and balance of payments effects, the dependency theory on the other hand views this kind of development as propagating capitalism in developed countries due to its benefits to the tourist generating economies. Citing the words of Milne (1990) he concludes that most of the goods and services required by the foreign tourists are imported into the developing countries from the developed countries (Batta, *op. cit.,* 45). In order to overcome the situation, he recommends ecotourism as an alternate form of tourism to avoid dependency.

However, the dependency theories have been criticised on three grounds. First, all important chains may not be in the hands of companies of the developed countries as is assumed in the dependency theory. Second, the theory analyses only the mass tourism phenomenon of international tourism and therefore does not take into account the low budget tourists or drifters. Third, it does not consider the domestic tourism (*ibid*).

Wahnschafft (1982), in his study of formal and informal tourism in Pattaya of Thailand, distinguishes both sectors based on the size of the business. According to him, the formal sector of tourism includes accommodation, restaurants, recreation centres and souvenir shops whereas the informal sector of tourism includes hawkers, street vendors, prostitutes and craftsman. But Michaud (1991) differentialtes both sectors by the size and organisation of the tourism business. The weaker part of these thories is their rather generalistic view of international tourism in those countries. They focus on the formal tourism sector and neglect the informal sector. This is a kind of one-sided analysis of urban economy. The most extreme case of formal torusim sector is the 'all-inclusive' package tours.

Propounding his hypothesis of formal and informal sector tourism, Oppermann (1993) argues that there is one factor common in all the above theories and that is that they neglect the phenomenon of drifter tourism. Although the tourists are divided into two groups, institutional and non-institutional tourists, only institutional tourists are analysed in research even though the differentiation of formal and upper circuit tourists and informal and lower sector tourists have vital socio-economic implications. The upper circuit tourism is characterised by high dependency on foreign exchange and low multiplier effects while the informal sector has a very high integration with the local economy (Batta, *op. cit.*, 46).

Citing the works of Kermath and Thomas, and Michaud and Wasnschafft, Oppermann states that these studies have applied the distinction of formal and informal sectors and have concluded that the formal and informal sectors compete with each other and government bias towards the formal sector will eventually lead to an extinction of the informal sector. Hence, the spatial occurrence and impacts of upper circuit tourism are limited to a restricted number of resorts, often in the vicinity of capital cities. The distribution of lower circuit is much wider, leakages are much lower and impacts on the regional economic structure much higher.

Characteristics of the Two Tourism Sectors

Characteristics	*Formal sector*	*Informal sector*
Capital	Abundant	Limited
Technology	Capital-intensive	Labour-intensive
Organisation	Bureaucratic	Primitive
Ownership	Companies	Individual, family
Prices	Generally fixed	Negotiable
Inventories	Large quantities and/or high quality	Small quantities and/or uneven quality
Fixed costs	Substantial	Neglibible
Advertisement	Necessary	Almost none
Credit	Institutional	Non-institutional
Turnover	Large	Small
Profit margin	Small per unit	Large per unit
Educaton	Skilled	Unskilled
Regular wages	Prevalent	Less prevalent
Government aid	Extensive	None or almost none
Dependence on foreign countries	Great, externally oriented	Small or none, often inward looking

Note: Adopted from Oppermann (1993)

The table given below summarizes such attempts to build theories of tourism development.

Noronha's Theory of Different Stages of Tourism

Stage 1	*Stage 2*	*Stage 3*
Discovery: Tourist Discovery of new destination	Local Response and Initiative: Local entrepreneurs provide facilities to accommodate growing tourist numbers.	Institutionalization: Mass tourism follows, take-over of development by organizations located outside local community

Source: (Noronha, 1973:16; 1977:17–27)

Peck and Lepie's Typology of Touristic Development

Rate of Change	*Power basis*	*Payoffs and tradeoffs Effects on Life-Style of Community*
Rapid Growth	"Bedroom" communities Summer residents, Specialized commerce (outside financing)	Rapid change of local norms new power structure and economy
Slow Growth	Individual developments local ownership expanding local commerce (local financing)	Slow change of norms, stable power structure, expanding local economy
Transient Development	Pass-through weekenders seasonal entrepreneurs (local financing)	Stable norms individual mobility within power structure and economy little overall change in local economy

Source: (Peck and Lepie, 1989:204)

Rodenberg's Scale of Tourism Development

Types of Development	*Scale of development (accommodation and tourist types)*	*Use of local resources and effect on traditional relationship*
Craft	Family owned and run, caters for independent travellers.	Entirely based on local resources traditional relationships remain largely unchanged.
Small Industrial	Average 21 rooms but up to 100, for independent travellers.	Some imports, traditional relationship still important, even if changing.

Types of Development	*Scale of development (accommodation and tourist types)*	*Use of local resources and effect on traditional relationship*
Large Industrial	100+ rooms, International standard hotels. Many extra facilities. Cater to package charter tourists.	Large import component. New industrial/ bureaucratic type relationships and values

Source: (Rodenberg, 1980:177–196: *see in* detail Cohen, 1984)

Cohen's Theory of Organic Development

Organic development potential	Initiated by locals in response to growing demand from tourists. with further development a possible shift from insider to outsider control.	Organic development more likely if: * local awareness of tourism * isolated from national society * strong and hostile local leaders * little infrastructure development * no large nearby urban centers
Induced development	Initiated by outsiders in an attempt to attract tourism to a new locality. With increasing development growing opportunities for locals, especially in provision of ancillary services.	Induced development less likely if as above

Source: (Cohen, 1983a: 158–162)

Smith's Seven Categories of Tourist

Types of tourist	*Number of Tourists*	*Community impact*
1. Explorer	Very limited	
2. Elite	Rarely seen	
3. Off-beat	Uncommon but seen	
4. Unusual	Occassional	Steadily
5. Incipient mass	Steady flow	Increasing
6. Mass	Continuous influx	
7. Charter	Massive arrival	

Source: Smith (1989:11–13)

Noronha's theory is a summary of much early tourism research and is unilinear in approach. The remaining others are all multilinear indications that different rates of growth and/or control over development have different implications for the host community (Wilson, 1993:41). Nevertheless, they provide an interesting range of variables with which to compare the situation. A study of Mahe Island revealed that the Island went almost directly from Noronha's stage to Cohen's theory of organic development (cited in Pradhan, 1998:6).

Doxey (1975) proposed an irritation index or 'irridex' to asses host–guest interactions and relationships. Doxey's scale has four steps; euphoria (delight in the contact), apathy (increasing in difference with larger numbers), irritation (concern and annoyance over price rise, crime, rudeness, cultural rules being broken) and finally antagonism (covert and overt aggression to visitors).

Another stage development model relating to tourism has been proposed by Butler (1980). In his model the impacts of tourism are not the direct focus of attention. Instead the model is concerned with the more general issue of the evolution of tourist areas (marketing issues, organisation and ownership of the tourist services and attractions), although the attitudes of residents and community support for tourism are discussed as a part of the larger process. Butler sees tourist areas as evolving through the stages of exploration, involvement, development, consolidation, stagnation and then either decline or rejuvenation. He has given six stages of resort life-cycle. In the consolidation stage he sees the emergence of social impacts. The large numbers of visitors and the facilities provided for them can be expected to arouse some opposition and discontent among permanent residents (*ibid*, 8), The stagnation phase where peak numbers of visitors have been reached is seen as follows: capacity levels for many variables will have been reached or exceeded with attendant environmental, social and economic problems (*ibid*). This model is based on product life-cycle concept widely used in business management.

Stage-based models of individual and social processes invite a number of criticisms, many of which can be directed at these tourism-related models. All three models have poor demarcation between the stages or steps. It is also unclear whether shifting from one stage to another precludes the continued existence of the previous stage. The Doxey and Smith models appear to assume this point but Butler notes that some tourist destinations (he cites the major Mexican resort of Cancun) may move directly into a higher level stage without the preceeding steps. Doxey and Butler models question is it the whole community which becomes hostile to tourism or are there only sections of the population who suffer and complain about the social impacts? And finally, one must query whether the whole process of social impacts and tourism evolution as outlined is inevitable, leaving individuals and local groups powerless to confront the forces of economic change and gain (Pearce, 1997:113–115).

Stage-based models of individual and social processes invite a number of criticisms, many of which can be directed at these tourism-related models. All three models have poor demarcation between the stages or steps.

Development of trekking tourism in Nepal seems to fit into a theoretical concept designed by Forster (1964), Cohen (1972) and Noronha (1977) which suggest that tourism development proceeds through three distinguishable stages.

The three-stage concept does not and cannot claim to deliver a general theory of touristic development. It serves rather as a descriptive model of a process. Its relevance for the discussion of the relationship between touristic penetration and development lies in the fact that it draws attention to two important pre-conditions for successfuly planned development. It first shows that the positive impact of policy measures depends on the right timing, respecting the largely irreversible character of touristic influence on local population and it emphasises, secondly, the importance of a clean perception of sound balance between touristic inflow and local absorbative capacity. The triviality of these findings stands in sharp contrast to the actual development of trekking tourism in Nepal (Baumgartner, 1986:213).

The tourism life-cycle concept and the carrying capacity concept are interrelated in a manner that is both dynamic and dependent. The life-cycle concept suggests that destination areas change over time, and progress through stages from introduction to decline. This reveals that the tourist caused tourism and tourism destroys tourism. But, in order to solve the problem, Schiffman has proposed growth management planning (extracted from Theobald, 1997:182–183).

In principle, tourism carrying capacity issues can be incorporated into the comprehensive planning agenda of most tourism destinations. Key to the success of such agendas is growth management programmes. Based upon a destination's ability to provide urban services and the vision of what growth rates should be encouraged, growth management plans offer a 'guidance system' to implement that vision (Schiffman, 1989). Growth management decision guides include policy statements, capital budgets and improvement programmes. Action instruments to support identified programmes encompass public investment strategies, land-use regulations and fiscal incentives or disincentives. They go beyond strictly land-use planning by incorporating other control mechanisms influencing tourism and other activities within the destination. Research in well-established tourism destinations suggests that growth management planning programmes can be effective management tools in addressing tourism impact issues. However, there appear to be few comprehensive applications of these approaches.

Tourism, therefore, is not only considered a positive influence on the economy, but it is seen as an instrument of development. However, to what extent tourism is an agent of development is an issue of empirical research. Several studies have indicated that tourism has largely remained confined to capital cities and important centers of economic activity. The immobility of tourists in the developing countries due to lack of infrastructure has led to the concentration of tourism infrastructure at only a few places. It is argued that opening of new international airports can lead to development of new infrastructure; however, it leads to conflicts in land use with agriculture not being able to compete with tourism. Moreover, if tourism is developed in backward regions, it will have very low backward linkages and therefore will not have any effect on the regions's development.

ACCULTURATION

Cultural effects of tourism and cultural tourism are not the same subject of anthropology. The former refers to changes in the elements of culture resulting from the presence and activities of tourism. As far as cultural tourism is concerned, Smith (1989:2–3) defined cultural tourism as 'the absorption by tourists of features resembling the vanishing lifestyles of past societies observed through such phenomena as house styles, crafts, farming equipment and dress'. Cultural aspects of tourism are considered to cover all those aspects of travel whereby people learn each other's ways of life and thought. Ritchie and Zins (1978:257) have defined as an element in the attractiveness of tourism regions. They isolated 12 elements of culture which attract tourists to the particular destinations:

(1) Handicrafts,

(2) Language,
(3) Traditions,
(4) Gastronomy,
(5) Art and Music, Concerts Paintings and Sculpture,
(6) History,
(7) Work and Technology,
(8) Architecture,
(9) Religion,
(10) Educational System,
(11) Dress and
(12) Leisure Activities.

Cultural tourism, by definition, is a force for cultural preservation. Lea (1988) presents three major elements of culture which attract visitors: Forms of culture which are inanimate or which do not directly involve human activity. Tourists visiting places of unique architecture and art, historical buildings and monuments, and purchasing traditional arts and crafts are notable examples; Forms of culture reflecting the normal daily life of a destination. Visiting 'foreign' peoples to observe their normal social, economic and leisure activities in an attempt to understand their lifestyle, ideologies and customs is a common tourist motivation; Forms of culture which are especially animated and may involve special events or depict historic or famous occurrences. Examples include musical festivals, carnivals, festivals reflecting old traditions and behavior, reenactments of battles and displays of old machinery.

The term acculturation refers to sociocultural change, desirable or not, that results from cultural contact. In practice, anthropologists, including those studying tourism, have tended to focus on acculturation involving more developed western peoples and less developed native population, which has mostly assumed some form of dominant–subordinate relationship. This was first sighted by Nunez (1963) and McKean (1976). Most studies and examples have shown a gradual weakening of traditional culture and what has been termed the development of a Coca-Cola society within indigenous life style (Shivji, 1973).

Anthropologists have been examining acculturation for decades, arguing that when contact takes place between a strong culture and a weaker one, it is usually that the former influences the latter. These studies have the underlying assumptions that cultural changes

(1) occur primarily in the indigenous society's traditions, customs and values rather than in the visiting group and
(2) are leading to a gradual homogenisation of cultures, in which the local identity is being assimilated into the stronger culture. (Modi, 2001:107).

The alternative concept of acculturation for the study of tourism is cultural drift. It represents a relatively new approach to the study of the cultural effects of tourism. The relationships are frequently of a seasonal, intermittent and multiple contact form marked by a cultural distance between the hosts and guests (Collins, 1978:278). According to the same author, cultural drift in this sense states that the role of the guest differs from that of the host and that the temporary contact situation results in change of phenotypic behavior in both the host and the guest. The phenotypic change may be permanent in the host society/ culture but temporary in the guest society/culture (Mathieson and Wall, 1982:162).

Cultural drift has turned the culture of some primitive, simple, host populations into 'Coca-Cola' cultures (Davidson, 1982:176; McKean, 1989:129), so that disco music, neon lights and cocktail bars begin to replace the traditional music and leisure activities of the host population. There can be also found linguistic acculturation in the host society. Nevertheless, while tourism can help to preserve the culture of a host population, more often the effects are harmful. One possible effect of tourism on culture is trivialisation, when aspects of the host culture become a degraded and commercialised form of entertainment for tourists (Davidson, 1989:169). The presence of 'stronger' western ideas and practices introduced by tourism means that the process is largely a kind of 'assimilation' of the 'weaker' host culture. But it does not mean that tourism will not work to revitalise the host's culture. While tourism is not the only factor which leads to cultural drift, the cinema and television being others, it can have the effect of accelerating the process (*ibid*, 176).

While describing the impact of tourism on culture, Turner and Ash (1975) write, 'the tourists superior economic wealth rapidly erodes the sensuous and aesthetic wealth of cultures that have developed in isolation from the western world'. This reveals that the consequences of tourism are harmful in the traditional society. But several studies have found positive effects of tourism on culture through the promotion of intercultural communication. Mobility, which is a prerequisite of tourism, is necessary for the contact of different social groups, nationalities and cultures. It has been argued that such contacts may contribute to the removal of social or national prejudices and the promotion of better understanding and positive social change. Evans postulated that cross-culture communications between tourists and hosts may promote adaptive changes in local culture while preserving or revitalising local ethnic and cultural identity. Actually it depends upon which types of tourists (see Cohen, 1972; Smith, 1989) are in the destinations, which kind of (the spatial, temporal and communicative context) contact takes place and what role is played by the cultural broker (the guide)?

Culture is a changing phenomenon which may occur as a result of

(i) modifications of the ecological niche occupied by a society. Changes to the habitat of a society often induce changes which may involve cultural adaptation and change.
(ii) contact between two societies with different cultures may bring about changes to both groups.
(iii) evolutionary changes occurring within a society.

This refers to the process of adaptation where societies change in response to internal biological and social needs to ensure satisfaction from their environment. Tourism could conceivably influence all three of these modes of change, but the literature on tourism documents the effects in the second category (Modi, 2001:107).

Much of the contemporary literature on the nature of modern tourism and its impact upon host societies relies on several important assumptions. In a most general way, these assumptions can be formulated as follows: First, tourism is said to lead to commoditisation of areas in the life of a community which prior to its penetration by tourism have been within the domain of economic relations regulated by criteria of market exchange (Greenwood, 1989). Local culture generally serves as the principal example of such commoditisation. In particular, 'colorful' local costumes, rituals and feasts, and folk and ethnic arts become touristic services or commodities as they come to be performed or produced for touristic consumption. The critical issue is whether commoditisation changes the meaning of cultural products and of human relations, making them eventually meaningless! (Modi, 2001:129).

Most anthropological investigations have been concerned with the effects of commercialisation on culture. This is mainly cited in the work of Graburn. With increasing exposure to the outside world, local cultures become 'pseudo native'. Anthropologists agree on the three major phases of change in traditional art forms resulting from outside contact:

(1) The disappearance of traditional artistic designs and art and craft forms particularly those with deep religious and mythical affiliations.

(2) This is followed by the growth of a degenerate, unsophisticated replacement which develops in association with mass production techniques.

(3) This is often followed by the resurgence of skill craftsmanship and distinctive styles incorporating the deeper cultural beliefs in the host society.

Deitch's study of the Indians of southwestern united states (Deitch, 1989) and Graburn's work with the eastern Canadian Innuit are clear examples of the positive effects of tourism on the arts and crafts of hosts.

Rogers (1983) interprets the process of diffusion as a transfer of innovation, and he categorises the social carriers of innovation according to their speed and degree of adoption of new or outside ideas. His categories are the innovative, the early adopters (the group which often includes the youth), the early majority, the late majority and the late adopters. The innovation spreads from a local place of origin or from an elite group of innovators to an ever-wider circle of regional or national adopters. The 'change agents' act as opinion leaders and are likely to come from the economic, political or cultural sectors (cited in Luger, 2000).

Chapter Three

TOURISM IN NEPAL

Using the language of the theorists mentioned above, it is interesting to see the position of Nepal. Tourism in Nepal has not yet progressed beyond Noronha's Stage 2. In Peck and Lepie's terms Nepal has shifted from transient growth to slow growth. In Rodenberg's terms Nepal is beginning to move from a craft to a small industrial type of tourism. Regarding Cohen's scheme Nepal provides with an example of organic development (Pradhan, 1998:7). While looking at the history of hotels, trekking agencies and travel agencies of Nepal, the first person to take the initiative in running a hotel was Mr. Boris Lissanevitch (Russian Nationality) who ran the Royal Hotel in Kathmandu in 1955 (Satyal, 1999:59). Likewise Takashi Miyahara (Japanese Nationality) opened the first Hotel Everest View in Khumbu at an altitude of 12000 ft. In Chitwan Mr. John Edward (British Nationality) started Tiger Tops in 1965. Similarly, the first travel agency named as Shah and Rai was established in 1959 at Hotel Coronation (Satyal, *op. cit.*, 75). It was Lt. Col. Jimmy Roberts (British) who first started trekking through Mountain Travel in 1964 (Satyal, 2000:192). This reveals that the foreign investors took the initiative in the field of tourism in Nepal and later the local entrepreneurs. The history shows that the conclusion drawn by Pradhan (1998:7) seems a little bit confused.

One worrisome note: Nepal may be heading towards more resort development that would probably be a mistake.

Whereas wildlife viewing and trekking build on what Nepal already has, resorts require—what it has not—roads, planes, imported fixtures and conveniences and they divert resources from the basic needs of citizens to the recreational comforts of leisure visitors. This is bad economics and in the long run it is bad politics (Ritcher, 2000:176).

According to Nepal Tourism Statistics 2000, the summary of total tourism is given below:

(1) Tourist arrivals: A total of 4,63,646 tourists visited Nepal during 2000 representing a decrease of 5.7% over the previous year.

(2) Arrivals by continent and nationality: Tourist arrivals to Nepal for the year were recorded as follows: 48.4% from Asia, 34.4% from western Europe, 10.1% from North America and 3.4% from Australia and Oceanic

The highest number of arrivals for 2000 was from India, comprising 20.7% of the total. This percentage, however, represents Indian tourists arriving in Nepal by air only.

The majority of tourists from overseas countries visiting Nepal were from Japan (8.9%), USA (8.7%), UK (8.1%) and Germany (5.7%) respectively. The arrival of overseas tourists recorded an increase of 4.8% in 2000 in comparison to 1999.

(3) Purpose of visit and length of stay: Although the largest number of tourists visited Nepal for recreational purposes (55.2%), adventure tourists posted the highest average length of stay in the country. The average length of stay was recorded as 11.9 days.

(4) Mode of Transport: Visitors entering by air constituted 81.3% of the total arrivals whereas 18.7% entered Nepal by land.

(5) Arrivals by sex and age: Male visitors comprised 57.6% of the total arrivals while female visitors accounted for 42.4%.

By age group, the highest share was recorded by the 31–45 age group followed by the 46–60 years group.

(6) Mountaineering: A total of 132 expedition teams were granted permission to scale different Himalayan peaks during 2000 out of which only 79 teams were successful in their attempt. The number of mountaineers was 773 while 11587 persons were employed by the expedition teams.

(7) Visitors to Pokhara and the National Parks: A total of 95,095 non-Indian tourists visited Pokhara, which comprised 25.9% of the total non-Indian travellers. Similarly 1,23,455 tourists visited different National Parks during 2000.

(8) Revenue from Tourism: Foreign exchange earnings from tourism stood at US$ 166.8 million which represented a decrease of 0.7% over the earnings of 1999. Contribution of tourism to the GDP of the nation was 3.1% and it also provided 12.9% of the total foreign exchange earnings during fiscal year 1999/00.

(9) Hotels and hotel rooms: The total number of tourist hotels recorded in 2000 was 848 of which 399 were based in Kathmandu valley and the rest in outstations like Pokhara, Chitwan, Nepalgunj, Birgunj, Dang, Bhairahawa and Palpa. The total number of rooms and beds available in these hotels were 18,203 and 34,958 respectively. Kathmandu accounted for 11,347 rooms with 21,297 beds where as hotels outside the valley accounted for 6,856 rooms with 13,661 beds. Thus in 2000 an increase of 8.0% in the number of hotels, 8.9% in the number of rooms and 8.5% in the number of beds was recorded.

(10) Trekking and Travel Agencies: The number of trekking and travel agencies recorded in 2000 were 537 and 637 respectively.

(11) Trekkers: A total of 1,18,780 trekkers were registered in 2000. Out of the total, 64.3% visited Annapurna area while those visiting the Everest and Langtang regions accounted for 22.5 and 9.2% respectively.

THE SETTING OF SAURAHA

Sauraha, a part of Bachhauli Village Development Committee, located in the close proximity of the Chitwan National Park, is connected to Tandi and Chitrasari villages by 6 and 3 km respectively. However, Tandi, the entry point to Sauraha is situated on the East–West National Highway, 5 km from the main city of Bharatpur. One can fly to Bharatpur from Kathmandu and then to Chitrasari by a bus or a car. It is also possible to go to Sauraha via Tandi and Chitrasari by a bus from Kathmandu along the Prithivi highway through Mugling, located midway to Pokhara, another tourist destination in Nepal. The distance from Kathmandu to the Chitwan National Park is 165 km and the road that connects them for the most part runs parallel to Trisuli River, a popular spot for whitewater rafting. In Tandi or Chitrasari the tourists making Sauraha their destination are taken by jeeps. It is also possible to visit Sauraha from India through the border towns of Birgunj and Bhairhawa in Nepal. Recently (in 2000 AD) three wheeler tempos have been operated from Tandi to Chitrasari. The Bacchhauli VDC comprises approximately 1500 households. The total population of this VDC is about 9696 (*Source:* VDC Secretariat). Temperature reaches a maximum of 45°C in May and a minimum of 0–6°C in December. Maximum rainfall recorded in the Park area is 216 mm, which is witnessed during September and October; the period between December and February is considered to be the best season for having a panoramic view of the park (Shrestha, 1994:38). This VDC comprises different villages such as Sauraha, Odra, Badreni, Malpur, Sisuwa, Padhariya, Mainaha, Dorangi, Bacchhauli, Janakauli, Jhuwani and Tarauli. There is a Police Post, Health Centre, Bank, Post Office, High School, Primary Schools, NGO's office and a big Osho Camp located at Bacchhauli. According to NIDS, there are altogether 4422 Tharus and the remaining other population (5244) is composed of Brahmins, Chhetris, Newars, Kamis, Gurungs, Magars, Tamangs, Botes, Damais, Danuwars and Dhobis in this VDC. The informants assumed that the majority of the households in this VDC hold an average of 1.5 *bigha* of land and approximately 15 houses hold above 5 *bigha* of land. River Budhi Rapti has divided VDC into three parts: Tandi, Chitrasari and Gothauli, all located on the northern side of the river. From the view point of tourism, Sauraha, Odra and Badreni villages are very important because most of the resorts are located there. The Tharu population of Sauraha village is approximately 200 and of Odra 220. Sauraha is occupied by 9 exogamous sub-groups whereas Odra is occupied by 13 exogamous sub-groups only. Further to the south of Sauraha there is a dense forest and near it, there are few Tharu villages like Patna, Dhindauli and Marchauli in Padampur VDC. Since the Rapti river for most part of the year remains swollen with rain water, it has isolated the village. Because of high level of water during monsoon period, (mid June–mid September) people of Padampur are isolated and have very little contact with the people of other village and localities. Padampur VDC had nearly 10,000 people from 1657 households in 1995 who used 345 species of plants as medicine, food fodder and fuel wood from the park (Yonzon, 2000:59). Under the relocation program, the population of Bankattha and Jayemangala villages is already relocated to Sagun Tole of the same district . Since the institution of Chitwan National Park in 1973, there have been considerable activities on the social and economic fronts in and around the village of Sauraha and this has brought transformations in socio-economic and cultural life and activities of the villagers. The present Sauraha gives a glimpse of today's Thamel of the Kathmandu valley, the lake side of Pokhara or Goa of India. Tourism in Sauraha is still on the second stage of Noronha (1977), Peck and Lepie (1989), Rodenburg (1980), and Cohen (1983a).

TOURISM IN SAURAHA

Tourism started in Chitwan in 1964 with a few hundred tourists per year (KMTNC, 1996:8–5). More recently Sauraha has become popular because it is located adjoining the Chitwan National Park. According to the data provided by the local sources, the Chitwan National Park is the third most important destination of tourists visiting Nepal. In 1992–93, the tourists visiting the National Park were 55,000. In the same year, roughly 23,000 tourists visited Sauraha excluding the number of tourists staying at the lodges inside the National Park. In 1997, out of 421,857 (Nepal Tourism Statistics, 1997:15) tourists visiting Nepal 92,717 (*ibid*, 16) visited Pokhara while 69,464 (*ibid*, 65) had visited the Royal Chitwan National Park. The number of tourists to RCNP has increased from 836 in 1974 (KMTNC, 1996:5-1) to over 69,464 in 1997. In this fiscal year, the revenue collected was

US $ 7,10,157. The number of lodges outside the Park has also increased during this period from about 10 in 1975 (KMTNC, *op. cit.*, 5–1) to 48 in 1997, which has provided employment and income opportunities to many people. The importance of Royal Chitwan National Park is increasing from the fact that the number of tourists visiting the National Park is on the rise. The majority of the tourists visiting the National Park are Europeans (70%) followed by North Americans (12%), Oceanic (12%) and Asians (6%) (KMTNC, *op. cit.*). The present volume of tourist flow in RCNP particularly in the Sauraha area appears to be reaching a limit. About two-thirds of the visitors surveyed perceived the problem of crowding or congestion in the existing infrastructure and environment management. Over 96% of the hotels surveyed also indicated that the area had already reached its full capacity and there was a need to limit the number of hotels in the future in Sauraha (KMTNC, *op. cit.*, 6–9). Tourism in Sauraha is still on the second stage of Noronha (1977), Peck and Lepie (1989), Rodenburg (1980), and Cohen (1983a).

HOTELS IN SAURAHA

Tourism plays an important role in the earning of national revenue but at the same time it has created earning sources for several local people and outsiders. If the outsiders who frequently came to Chitwan (for hunting) were exclusively 'VIPs' now-a-days it is people on 'package holiday' and low budget travellers. The tourists landed on the small landing strip near Meghauli, which had been constructed in 1961 on the occasion of the visit of the British Queen Elizabeth (Muller-Boker, 1999:54). The first non-commercial lodge was built at Kasara in1939 for the visit of King George VI of England. This lodge was the first building in the Terai to be made of concrete (Mishra and Jefferies, 1991:157). The first safari hotel opened in 1965 even before the national park had been created. Now, there are seven hotels out of which Tiger Tops is the oldest one and it came up before the establishment of the National Park. Tiger Tops including other hotels like Island Jungle Resort, Chitwan Jungle

Lodge, Gainda Wildlife Camp, Temple Tiger and Machan have played an important role in bringing a large number of quality tourists and earning a huge amount of foreign currency from the package program i.e. 2 nights/3 days = US $ 150–400 per person. Regarding the lodge characteristics and hotel accommodation and food the report of KMTNC shows the reality of Sauraha. According to the same report, for the purpose of the analysis, hotel/lodges (hereafter hotel and lodges are used interchangeably) are categorised on the basis of package tour price they had charged: expensive hotel (EH), moderately priced hotel (MPH) and low budget hotel (LBC). The average cost of the package tour charged by EH, MPH and LBC during the course of the survey were US $ 180–93 and 48 respectively. Majority of the lodges were LBC (56%) followed by MPH and EH (11%) (1996:5–4). Hotel accommodations and food charge for individual tourists varied by type of hotel. The average room rate with attached bathroom ranged from NRs. 300 in EH, with the overall average being about NRs. 670 per room per visitor. No EH surveyed had rooms without attached bathroom and such rooms were mostly found in MPC and LBC. The average charge for such room facilities ranged from NRs. 125 in LBC to NRs. 180 in EH, with overall average being NRs. 120 per tourist. But no effort has been made for developing other new products for increasing the tourist length of stay.

In Sauraha, there was only one simple lodge in 1977. In 1993 there were 48 hotels. Now, there are already 52 hotels/lodges registered at Hotel Association of Sauraha in 1999. The average accommodation capacity of the hotels was of 16 beds or eight huts. Recently, Sapkota (2000:56) has mentioned 54 hotels/lodges to have 585 rooms and 1055 beds. The price variation of accommodation in Sauraha is found to range from US $ 2 to US $ 25 for a single bedroom and US $ 3 to US $ 35 for a double bedroom. More than 48% of visitors visiting RCNP spend less than US $ 50 and on an average, tourists visiting Sauraha spent US $ 67 on lodging, fooding and other park activities in their stay in Sauraha. Roughly 58% of total visitors are found to stay for 2 days and only 3% of visitors were found to stay more than 5 days. The hotels outside the Park are currently making a limited income. There should be no further expansion of lodges in the Sauraha area and their upgrading in terms of better facilities and services will help improve their incomes (KMTNC, 1996:8-5).

The lodges in Sauraha signify huge investment. Lodge owners are of the opinion that investment in lodges was giving good return in the past when there were not many lodges and competition among the lodge owners was not very stiff. Presently, competition is high. There is no regulation regarding the rates being charged. Although there are two associations (Hotel and Community Development Committee and Hotel Association of Nepal-Chitwan Chapter) of the hotel owners, they are not effective. There is undercutting about the rates and in few cases the room rents even come down to NRs 100 per night. Even good lodges and resorts of this village do not have much business because their promotional activities are very unsatisfactory while the lodges which provide low quality services have a big volume of business on account of their good promotional activities and advertisements. The competition among the lodge owners has become more intense nowadays and it will be even more in the future because of new resorts under construction. The types of lodges vary from the big and sophisticated ones. It has been estimated from the study (Pandey *et. al*, 1993) that total investment in lodges/resorts in Sauraha district comes up to around NRs. 500 million.

However, in the context of development of tourism in Sauraha, the luxrious hotels like Baghmara Resort, Chitwan Resort Camp, Hotel Hermitage Boat House, Royal Park, Jungle Camp, Jungle Safari Lodge, Rhinos Residency, Green Mansions, Gaida Wildlife Camp are already operational. Previously, most of the resorts had traditional Tharu hut type with thatched roofs, but after 1994, most of the traditional huts have been replaced by concrete buildings, and also the thatched roofs have been replaced by zinc plates. This reveals that already there is architectural pollution in Sauraha. One major advantage of having thatched roofs is that every year grass has to be added on the roof. This requirement, which need addition of grass annually on the roofs of the resorts, generates income to the local people. It is estimated that small resorts require roughly NRs. 25,000 annually to repair the roof while the bigger one requires about NRs. 60,000. Some resorts have roofs which are unique in shape and these cannot be repaired by the local people. The major part of expenditure made by the resort owners on the maintenance of roofs goes to the villagers. The raw material (grass) used for the maintenance of the roofs is procured from the local forests (Pandey et al., 1993).

The Indian, Taiwanese, Hong Kong and Singaporean tourists prefer to stay in the rooms having sufficient modern facilities whereas the western tourists love to stay in the hotels which are in fact the cottages of traditional style. Considering the influx of the Singaporean, Hong Kong, Indian and Taiwanese tourists, and also examining the aspect of safety of their articles, the lodge-owners of Sauraha have now started the construction of cemented buildings for their accommodation. The tourists visit certain areas to enjoy the traditional culture and environment, which often contributes in the growth of tourism of a given region. Some observers opine that after the complete shift in the building activities in Sauraha and array of modern buildings, as well as changed cultural context, in the future too there is bright hope of tourism.

As far as the nature of development of tourism inside and outside the park is concerned, enclave development inside the park and integrated development outside the park is found. '... enclave tourism is sometimes adopted as a deliberate policy by a host country, in order to limit tourism's cultural or environmental impacts' (Ceballos-Lascurian, 1996:13; Picard, 1995). In enclave tourism, backward linkages are very weak, especially if the enclaves are controlled by multinational interests (McKee, 1988, cited in Ceballos-Lascurian, 1996:13). 'Enclavism, can for instance create a "them" and "us" type syndrome. Price enclavism can exclude the host community and present an unachievable lifestyle and thus create resentment in the host community. Integrated development, on the other hand, while being small-scale and community oriented, can lead to greater contact between tourists and hosts which at peak times may lead to friction and misunderstanding' (Jackson, 1989:120).

The phenomenal development of tourism in Sauraha is also due to the location factor, which further assisted the sub-urban growth of the destination. Sauraha, the close proximity of RCNP, attracted a number of visitors which greatly enhanced the development of modern resorts or hotels and other servicing infrastructures. As a result, the Sauraha village, formerly unexposed village, is now converted into a most popular location of tourist resorts with highly standard hotels, restaurant and other facilities. With the growth of tourism in Sauraha the land value has been increased. A number of industries flourished, specially hotel industry, fruit farming, vegetable farming, poultry farming and livestock farming (Sapkota, *op. cit.*).

TOURISM TARIFF AND QUALITY SERVICE

When a tourist lands in Kathmandu, he has several alternatives: innercity tour, mountain flight, trekking, whitewater river rafting and jungle safari. When a tourist decides to make his destination to the Chitwan National Park he is likely to spend a minimum of 2 nights/3 days. The destination offers Tharu Stick Dance, Village Tour, Bird Watching, Elephant Ride, Jungle Drive, Ox Cart Ride, Sunset View, Elephant Breeding Center Tour, Elephant Stable Tour, Jungle Walk, Night Walk, Tower Night, Swimming Program, Meditation Program, Machan Night Program, Bicycle Visit to 20,000 lakes, Churia Hill Trek and Canoe Trip. Package programs to Sauraha are usually sold by the Kathmandu located Safari Agents. The package tour is generally for 2 nights and 3 days. It was found from the field survey that there is almost uniformity on the tariffs for Sauraha except in case of few standard resorts, or for those which cater for low income tourists. According to the general tariffs of Sauraha, a tourist is charged US $ 90 for 2 nights and 3 days. In this cost entrance fee to the park, the elephant ride or jungle drive, food, accommodation, cultural program (Tharu stick dance) and other activities in the resort is included.

On the way to Sauraha after reaching Chitrasari, immediately after getting down from the bus he finds himself surrounded and harassed by hotel agents. Each agent tries to allure the tourist to choose the resort that he/she is representing. Even those tourists who have their reservations from Kathmandu are also harassed in the beginning. It is a common sight and for this most of the tourists are highly confused. The tourists visiting Nepal for the first time are found more confused. However, for those foreign tourists who come to Nepal through India, it is not a new scene. In 1993 as it was observed in Tandi that for one tourist there were more than 20 hotel agents each trying to persuade the tourist to come to their resort. Resort owners reported that when the tourist finally reaches the resort they receive only around $ 50. Roughly 40% of the money the tourist pays for the trip get leaked out in the form of discounts to different people involved right from the taxi driver taking him from the airport to the city to the agents selling different products in Kathmandu. It has been estimated that a resort which charges $ 90 from a tourist to visit Sauraha for 2 nights and 3 days, in fact gets about $ 50 only and from that he has to meet all the expenses. On an average a resort is found to make a net profit of NRs. 500 ($ 10) per tourist for the two nights and three days package (Pandey et al., 1993). From this kind of receipt, the quality of services offered to the tourist at Sauraha will not be standard because the resort owners do not get the prices they quote. Prices vary from resort to resort. On account of high competition among them there is often 50% reduction in the prices. It has been found that the price of the bus ticket from Kathmandu to Chitrasari also varies and the tourists pay that owing to their ignorance of the fact. Tourism to Sauraha is also found to be highly disorganised.

Chapter Four

THE CHITWAN NATIONAL PARK AND ITS IMPACT

The Chitwaniya Tharus' neighboring forest was declared a hunting reserve in 1963. In 1973 His Majesty Late King Mahendra approved it as the first National Park because of its potential of environment for Rhinoceros and Tiger preservation. The Royal Chitwan National Park is spread over 932 sq. km dominated by *kathaban* or *jinawahan* (sal forest-*Shorea robusta*), riverine forest comprised *sissohan* tree *(Dalbergia sissoo)*, *simarhani* tree *(Bombax ceiba)*, *jhaksihani*—the savannas of tall grass *(Saccharum spontaneum)* swampy areas called *dhab* and *gaheri*. (Muller-Boker, 1999). The Tharus of Chitwan easily distinguish the surrounding 'ecotope' (plant community) and 'biotope' (a forest canopy or a portion of a habitat characterised by uniformity in climate and distribution of biotic and abiotic components) on the ground of ecological conditions (Muller-Boker, 1991a). In 1983 Chitwan National Park was enlisted as a World Heritage Site. The park is (roughly 100 km long and 40 km wide) located in tropical and subtropical climatic region with an altitudinal range of 800–1500 m. It contains a dominant sal forest (about 70%), grassland (about 25%), lakes (17%), rivers (3%) and a large number of species (56 mammals, 47 reptiles, 500 birds, 9 amphibians, 120 fish (Shrestha, 1999:101) and 570 flower plants (RESOURCES NEPAL, 1999) of different kinds.

In the vicinity of Sauraha, there is one INGO known as

King Mahendra Trust for Nature Conservation (KMTNC). Program wise, the activities undertaken by the Trust can be broadly grouped into the following categories: Natural Resource Conservation; Conservation Education and Extension; Impact Study and Advocacy Services and Sustainable Community Development. However, resource conservation and management through community participation ensuring sustainable development is the major thrust of the Trust (Bajracharya and Thapa, 2000:284).

About a decade after the establishment of RCNP, the Trust established the Nepal Conservation Research and Training Center (NCRTC) in Sauraha on the fringes of the national park with the objective of carrying out applied biological research: Rhino and Tiger Monitoring/Census, Ungulate/Bird/Bison Survey, Vegetation and Habitat Analysis and Research grant to students; Socio-economical Research: Tourism Impact Survey, Natural Resource Use Survey, and Micro-enterprise Survey; Training: Wildlife Techniques, Community Participation, Community Forestry Conservation Education, Nature Guide and Hotel and Lodge Management; Buffer Zone Management: Buffer Zone plantation and Habitat Extension, Buffer Zone by laws and Formation of Stakeholder Committee Community Development: Community Health Service, Vegetable Co-operatives and School Support (*ibid*, 285–289).

There is a Ghadiyal Centre at Kasara which was started in 1978 as a project and begun functioning from 1981. Since Ghaddiyal is a endangered species it is being reared at this centre. In this park there is also a visitor centre, souvenir shop, museum, seven lodges and four tented camps. Crop raiding, livestock depredation and loss of lives are associated with the spill-over of growing population of large mammals from the park (RESOURCES NEPAL, 1999).

Every year the park is opened for the villagers so that they are able to collect the products they need from the forests. The villagers collect grass, firewood and other forest products. It is from the forests that the grass for the roofs is procured. The parks usually open for a few days each year between mid-January to the first week of February.

Number and values of thatch reed grass collection permits 75, 143 (1996/97) generated US $ 5,571 (1 US $ = NR $ 68). In 1992, for the first time the villagers were permitted to collect firewood from the forests. When the parks are opened, even schools are closed so that the villagers along with their family members and school-going children can avail the opportunity to enter the forests to collect forest products. The grass that is obtained from the forests is sold to the lodges/resorts for the repair of roofs. Presently, the new resorts that are being constructed use corrugated sheets as roofing material. Again, there has been a drastic change in the method of construction in new resorts.

The most successful enterprise, without any doubt, is the national park itself. In the fiscal year 1989/90 the park had an income of US $ 4,48,330, comprising 65.4 admission fee, 14.4% elephant ride charges, 12.2% hotel licences and 7.9% miscellaneous. In contrast the expenses only amounted to US $ 81,578 (IUCN, 1993:369). Thus more than 80% of the income was channeled to Kathmandu, a very lucrative business for the state (Muller-Boker, 2000:112).

Regarding entry fee to the park and community forest, elephant ride, government has increased the rate effectively from May, 2000. According to the new policy, the foreign, Indian and Nepalese visitor is charged NRs 1000, 600, and 220 respectively for elephant ride inside the park. As far as entrance fee to the park is concerned, every western tourist has to pay NRs 500 which is valid for only 1 day. Those western and Indian tourists who visit community forest can use the same permit for 2 days that is valid for only 1 day in the park. In order to make canoe trip inside or outside park, each individual foreign tourist including Indian is charged NRs 230, and NRs. 50 for Nepalese visitor. In order to drive a jeep inside the park, the owner has to pay NRs 2000 for permit. Those tourists who take an interest to go for a jungle drive have to pay NRs 700 to the jeep owner on individual basis. The carrying capacity of the jeep will be a minimum of 7 and a maximum of 10 persons. Jeep drive will be conducted twice a day, i.e., once in the morning from 7 a.m. to 12 noon and then from 1 to 5.30

p.m. One can go for jungle drive either in the morning or in the afternoon. In the same way, the elephant ride is also conducted inside the park twice a day, i.e., once in the morning and then in the afternoon. But, the duration of ride will be only an hour.

The forest is one of the major parts of nature that affects man and his culture. For survival, man needs food, clothing, shelter, fuel and climate heating. Forest ecosystem for centuries has been inextricably bound with the life of Tharu community.

In the context of the Tharus of Chitwan and their association with nature, Muller-Boker (1999) writes, the Tharus are closely related to nature and the world of spirits. Environmentally, their habitat was totally uncontaminated. Their traditional form of livelihood and economic activity was oriented towards exploitation of forests and grasslands. Until the 1950s agricultural economy was based on shifting cultivation. The forest and grasslands, together with rivers and streams, were also pasturage for their large herds of cattle as well as being hunting, fishing, and gathering grounds; they provided all the firewood and the raw materials necessary for house construction and household items, it is the Tharus who have been affected by the loss of these forests and grassland areas so important to their way of life. Earlier the forest was a part of their livelihood and economy. It was a way of life and the part of their cultural identity.

'... the Tharus highly revere the forest as the place where the Gods and spirits live. For them it is that much harder to confront the ideas of Western ecologists who see the forest and the savannas only as a living space for animals, one in which the Tharus no longer have a place'. The pantheon of Tharu Gods exhibit a large number of deities that live in the forest, and they may feel disturbed by the inappropriate behavior of intruding humans. Even more dangerous are the spirits (*bayar*), whose paths one may accidentally cross. The Tharus avoid these 'spirit ways' (*bah*); the shaman knows where the spirits and Gods abide (usually in damp places and puddles). Before going into the forest, one recalls the name of the forest deities and asks them for their aid; in the forest avoids doing 'bad things' (*ibid*). As mentioned above, the Tharus had a close relationship with the nature (cultural ecology) and spirit (supernatural forces) world. This kind of relationship is coined as nature (cultural ecology) man (social system) spirit (supernatural force) complex (see in Kunwar, 1989). The life style of the Tharus changed drastically when the National Park came into being. There were rules and regulation set by the Park authorities and the Tharus who were so closely associated to nature and the land surrounding it were left helpless. There was a kind of communication gap between them and nature which was part of their life. Their very life and existence was challenged and changed. Agriculture and animal husbandry being their way of survival was greatly affected by conservation. Having no other alternative the ethnic group suffered more than one could imagine. Except for the yearly grass cutting permits to about 60,000 local people, little benefits has flowed from tourism and conservation. Thus, for survival they have to illegally enter the Park for firewood and fodder, and if caught in the process they are penalised (KMTNC, 1996:1–3).

Since the forest was declared as Park, neither are they allowed to hunt wild animals for food nor can they collect grass from the National Park during the time of festivals and religious activities. Because of the lack of pasture, the inhabitants of this area are unable to keep many animals. This has affected them immensely. Similarly, they have stopped collecting traditional medicinal plants, jungle fruits and vegetables, which is affecting the nutritional value of their diets. They feel it is very difficult to catch fish and snails, which is their staple food, and a necessity for their festivals. Thus, the nature–man–spirit complex of the Tharus is becoming weaker. As far as the Tharu house is concerned, the style and design have also changed because of the restrictions they are unable to collect the necessary materials from the forest area. The whole material culture was made by locally available forest-product but now it is also changed. They have also lost their tradition of shifting cultivation. The loss of a nomadic life-style has forced them to stay in one place and therefore, the impacts of wildlife destroying crops is much greater in their habitat. Thus the conservation policy has induced the Tharu's cultural survival (McLean, 1997–98).

COMMUNITY FOREST, TOURISM AND DEVELOPMENT

The community development programs run by the Center (NCRTC) are designed to assist the people living in the villages within the buffer zone of the park. These community programs include community forestry, micro enterprises, women development, local skill development, health, sanitation and conservation education. In the past 5 years, the Center has been able to extend the community forestry program in more than 1500 hectares and it has been proved successful in providing fuel, fodder, timber and grass requirement of over 10,000 people living around the park. A new approach of community forestry interlined with ecotourism activities to generate income for local communities, developed and launched recently by the Center in two Village Development Committees of Chitwan (Bacchauli and Kumrose) with support from the Biodiversity Conservation Network, USA, has been very successful. The project has not only been able to address the local demand for forest products, thus reducing the pressure inside the park, but has also been providing handsome income from tourism. Another attractive feature of the community plantations is that it is not simply guided by the objectives of aforestation but also incorporates concept of habitat restoration (Bajracharya and Thapa, *op. cit.*, 288).

There are three community forests known as Baghmara Community Forest, Janakauli Community Forest and Kumroj Community Forest. First two community forests lie in Bachhauli VDC and the third one lies in Kumrose VDC. The first one is located at Ward No. 1 and extends up to Ward No. 4. The second one is located at Wards 5–9. The third one is located in Kumroj VDC. Since Buffer Zone by-laws was approved in 1996, 30–50% of the parks' revenue flows directly to the communities for development and conservation activities. A stakeholder committee has been formed comprising VDC chairmen, district forest officers, hotel representatives and RCNP and KMTNC officers to identify the needs of the local communities and provide local support to the conservation of RCNP (Beun and Lamichhane, 1999:25). In October 1996, tourism was introduced in Baghmara Forest Community, as Jangle walk and elephant ride in the National Park was in demand by quite a lot of tourists.

To take the private elephants in Baghmara Community Forest, the owners have to pay a deposit of NRs. 15,000 in the beginning. The tourists are generally sent to Baghmara and Janakauli Community Forest for elephant ride. In order to go to Kumroj Forest one has to go via Janakauli Forest. The elephant ride is managed by syndicate. The syndicate governs to the Hatti Unique and Hatti United Committees. Each Private elephant owner has to register with either of the two committees. The syndicate has managed a queue system of carrying the tourists to the community forest. Altogether the private elephant owners have 16 elephants. The Baghmara Community Forest comprises few Ward villages like Badreni (Ward No. 1), Sauraha and Odra (Ward No. 2), Malpur, Makbudi, Sishuwar and Mushihar Tole (Ward No. 3) and Mainaha and Padhariya (Ward No. 4). Altogether there are roughly 500 households. The community forest collects maximum revenues from the tourists; in return to this privilege, it has launched some developmental programs for the local community of those mentioned Wards of Bachhauli VDC. The money collected in their community fund has been used for Gravelling of the road; Building schools with the help of National Park, Hotels, Private enterprises and even tourists; Bee-keeping program implemented—loans given to the local people to implement bee-keeping program for their livelihood; Establishing Biogas bank; Knitting and sewing skills development classes provided to the females and also helped them in credit if they are interested in continuing it as their earning; Introducing Micro-credit program—5 lakh revolving fund (*ibid*, 27). Tourism is currently generating 25 lakhs for the local community. Now it has become a model project between the Park and People project of UNDP.

There are 20 elephants at Park and People Project. But the Project provides only 10 elephants for tourists' activities inside the Park. The elephants are hired by the tourists to explore the forests. Elephant rides are a great attraction for the tourists. In 1999, the lodge owners of Sauraha brought 11 elephants from India. The cost of one elephant is about Rs. 6,00,000. Those who have brought on lease, pay NRs. 6000–10,000 on monthly basis. Previously, the elephant ride was provided only by the national park. Because of the influx of tourism in Sauraha, it was very difficult to get the ticket for elephant ride inside the National Park. Now the lodge owners too provide elephant to the tourists outside the Park. If the elephant is sent to the community forest, the entrance fee per head is NRs. 50. For this ride, each tourist has to pay NRs. 600–650 to the lodge owners or any agent. Altogether, four persons will pay NRs. 2400–2600. From this amount, NRs. 1600 (including community forest fee as mentioned above) will go to the owner of the elephant. Although there is a great loss of revenue to the government, there is balance between the entrepreneurs because the lodge owners are also benefitted from the new management of elephant outside the park on one side, and the tourists' demand of elephant ride has been fulfilled on the other. On an average, one elephant will make a tour to the community forest four times a day in the season. In this way the structure of the touristic activities in Sauraha has been changed from the past.

Chapter Five

EMPLOYMENT

One of the most ubiquitously noted effects of tourism is its impact on the division of labor, particularly between the sexes. By creating new kinds of employment, tourism draws into the labor force parts of the local population previously outside it—specifically, young women who now find employment either in tourist services, such as hotels (Noronha, 1977:65); in the production of crafts and souvenirs for the market (Boissevain, 1979:83–84; Swain, 1977); or in tourism-oriented prostitution (Cohen, 1984:386). Though Davidson *(op. cit.)* is not in a position to recognise tourism as an industry, the others have recognised it as a multifaceted industry that directly affects sectors in the economy (hospitality, transport, local art and craft, building industry, food suppliers etc.) and indirectly affects many others. Another economic factor in tourism employment is its seasonal nature, causing fluctuating employment levels and short-term employment as well as long-term jobs. Rural workers whose work is seasonal may also find additional supplementary work in the tourism industry. Often the tourist season occurs during the rural off-season. Tourism, however, does bring many more non-pecuniary benefits than other export industries, for example, the upgrading of public facilities, parks and recreation areas, contact with other cultures and improved entertainment. Finally tourism is a decentralised industry that can be undertaken on a regional basis throughout a country. As stated before regional tourism is responsible for many social benefits by supporting family and village units and bringing economic activity to an area (Jackson, 1989:123–124).

Tourism in Sauraha has been an important employment generator. Employment ranges from the manpower working for the lodges/resorts to those working in the Wild Life Park, and others engaged directly or indirectly in the tourist sector. The industries have been employing local youths. However, it is interesting to note that the salary pattern of employees is low and the employees having relatively higher salary patterns are from outside the local area. In aggregate it is obvious that tourism in Sauraha plays vital role for employment opportunities for local people; market for local products; permanent source of foreign currencies earnings for country as well as for local people (Sapkota, op. cit.). One advantage of people working in the tourist sector in Sauraha is that for all these people it may be a secondary source of employment. It was reported that the literacy level till high school level is high. After SLC most of the students leave their studies and try to get employment in tourism business like naturalists, managers, cooks, housekeeper, boy, shop-owners etc., as it is an easy way of earning for them, contrary to the hardship that they would have to go through while farming with no exposure.

Employment in the lodges ranges from guide work to cooking, taking care of the dining rooms and working as room boys. A number of standard resorts have given permanent jobs to the Tharu women for laundry on a salary basis. The resort which has hired the women for the same work give Rs. 80 on daily wages basis. Washing clothes and taking care of the laundry is confined only to women. With the exception of laundry work there is no other kind of employment for women (Pandey et al., 1993). The picture is equally bad in gender analysis of employment in tourism. Sinclair (1997) has found that most of the top jobs in tourism sector of developed and developing countries are filled by men while ladies are employed on seasonal or part-time jobs only. Nevertheless the tourism sector is credited with opening up new job avenues for women in some of the developing countries like Barbados and Sri Lanka (Bhatta, 2000:57). There are some hotels run by family members where the father works as MD, the wife works as cook and the son works as naturalist. However, tourist activities around the Chitwan National Park have a favourable economic impact. There is high local employment because of the lower salaries in comparison to Kathmandu and Pokhara. Thus the local employment has been well generated in Sauraha and its periphery. Apart from local employment, a chain of other local Tharu are less benefited in comparison to the hill migrants. Nevertheless, tourist expenditures are found to be going in the pockets of local people.

In Sauraha, out of 200 people only 3 persons were found working at hotels in 1993. One person of the village is presently running a restaurant. Hotels are also run by three Tharu families. Other two families are running their mobile shops and one family is running a pub at the riverside. One of the villagers works as guide, one as driver, and one does the work of an overseer. Two families being landless have left the village. In Odra, out of 220 people, 2 work as drivers, 1 woman as washer woman, 1 runs a guide office, 3 people work as guides and 1 does the work of a cook. In this village, one young person of about 24 years has passed the I. Com. examination and a few boys have completed their studies up to class ten. Five boys have gone to India for their better fortune.

From the survey it was difficult to estimate the exact number of guides working at Sauraha. All the lodges have at least one guide because guides are very important. The statistics based on the number of guides trained shows that several guide training courses were conducted at KMTNC. The estimate puts that the number of guides trained in Sauraha is approximately 160 in 1995. Among them, approximately 40 guides are employed at the lodges and 25 work as freelance guides. The nature of tourism in Sauraha reveals that guides are very essential. All the tourist activities with the exception of elephant ride need guides.

Another important type of employment is jeep driving,

Till 1985–1987, most of the tourists visiting Sauraha used to travel by bullock carts or by elephants from Tandi to Sauraha (6 km). These days bullock carts and elephants have been completely replaced by jeeps. Jeep transportation has created employment for the jeep drivers. Most of the resorts have got a jeep. Approximately 40 persons work as jeep drivers. Jeep transportation is not only essential for bringing tourists from Tandi or Chitrasari to Sauraha but also for jungle drives. Recently a few resort owners have introduced *tanga* (horse cart).

Canoe ride is operated by Hotel Association under the contract system of National Park. In the fiscal year 1992/93 the hotel association was supposed to pay NRs. 220,000 to the National Park, although the total earning from canoe activity amounted to NRs. 600,000 for the same period. Mostly the Tharus row canoes in the river Rapti. In a day, an average of nine canoes are found carrying tourists to see the crocodiles and the elephant breeding centers. In 1992, there were 11 canoes operating in the river for tourists. Two men are employed to row the canoes. The capacity of a canoe is 2–10 tourists. Since canoe ride is a very important activity, almost every one in Sauraha has learned to row a boat. A boatman draws Rs.1500 per month as his salary. Generally the Tharus, fishermen (Bote) and potters (Kumals) are engaged in this activity. These days (in 1999) the canoe trip is operated outside the National Park also.

The large hotels employ a considerable number of laborers. The total employment in different lodges is estimated to be around 400–500. According to its own records, Tiger Tops employed some 400 people in 1983 during the peak season (Gurung, 1983:165). Within Sauraha premises, the maximum employment was found in Gaida Wild Life Camp which has employed 110 persons. The same kind of employment is also found in different lodges of inside the Park. The average employment for each resort located outside the park is 10 people. Since the minimum salary range is quite low, NRs. 800 per month, the majority of people employed are local only. The top management employees of the resorts are from Kathmandu. The guides do not seem to be working permanently at the same resort. The reason of shifting from one lodge to another is that the guides do not seem satisfied with the given salary. Very few resorts have developed a corporate culture (Schneider and Barsoux, 1997) in Sauraha.

Apart from the resorts being important employment generators, a whole series of activities catering for the tourists within the Sauraha village has provided opportunity for more people to work. The Sauraha village, apart from having lodges has a laundry shop, several Guide Centers, six rooftop restaurants, bicycle and motor-bike hiring centers, twenty-five mobile shops, four grocery shops, barber's hair cutting center, one medicine shop, few riverside pubs, souvenir shops, book shops, local tea shops, chicken house, one big Osho Camp and other residential buildings. Apart from these shops, seasonal vegetables are made available in the lodges by a contractor. There is also a vendor who procures vegetables from Tandi and supplies to the resorts and restaurants. The biggest contractor of the village reported that he supplies 180 kg of vegetables each day from October to March. After April the supply drops to 50 kg per day. Very little vegetables are cultivated in Sauraha. This was mainly because of labor shortage.

Most people of the village work on daily wages and are called *baniyara*. These people either work in the fields or in the hotels. The lodge owners use them for preparing fences, roofs and for cutting grass of the hotels. They also work as carpenters in the village. By nature, Tharus are very sincere and honest. They do not argue about anything and assiduously follow the rules given by the community. Although they know the importance of tourism, due to the lack of education and knowledge of foreign languages, they are not in a position to communicate directly with the tourists. Because of their low economy they can not run restaurants and hotels. They hold the view that tourism is good for those people who are educated, rich and farsighted. In this regard, some questions were asked to the non-Tharu residents of Sauraha about why the Tharus have not economically benefitted from the tourism industry.

The etic version was that they just want to eat and drink a lot. The etic version has been supported by the emic version. This reveals that the Tharus are extravagant specially on festive food and drink. They do not want to learn more from others and are not innovative in character. They are satisfied with their existing home and given environment. When they get money from somewhere they want to spend a big portion on alcohol and entertaining their relatives. Their women, often at the time of leisure, go to the riverside for fishing. Most of the male members go to the forest to collect firewood. In winter people sit together around the fireplace for a long time. In the summer (May–June) they are often found sitting along with their family members in light costume. It does not mean that they do not work at all. During this time, the non-Tharus are not seen outside their homes. The road remains empty for the whole day. In summer the Tharus work only in the morning and mobility starts in the evening when it is cool. During this season there will be very few tourists in Sauraha.

During field work in 1993, some young boys of Odra reported that they do not like to work in the hotel because there they do not get more than 500 Rs. per month. With this salary they cannot afford their livelihood. Therefore, they generally work as *baniyara*. From this, one earns a minimum of 1500 Rs. per month. In Odra, there are 5 boys who work as carpenters. From the view point of their livelihood, their condition has not changed from the past. Economically, they are exactly the same as before if not better. This does not mean that the majority of Tharus are frustrated with the growing tourist environment of the area. They are by nature shy, modest and quiet people.

Comparatively the outsiders and the non-resident Tharus of Sauraha have highly benefited from the tourism industry than the real residents of these two villages. The main reason of economic gap between the natives of Sauraha, the hosts and the tourists lies in the package program there. As mentioned earlier, these villages have become the centers of attraction to the tourists but the local residents are not getting any economic benefit from the tourist industry. Few Tharus expressed the view that their area is ultimately going to be dominated by the outsiders who have come to run the lodges there.

Agriculture still plays an important role but since the majority of people in and around Sauraha are engaged in the tourist sector there is a serious shortage of labor force in agriculture. This is particularly true with the big landlords. Those big landlords who have land in the vicinity of Sauraha have a big problem of labor shortage. Most of the landlords are found to rent out their land to the local people. The Report of KMTNC (1996) shows that economic impacts of tourism on household income is found to be minimal and limited to a small pocket of Bachhauli VDC despite the potential of diversifying tourism to different pockets. Less than 2% of the sample households were found to be employed directly by tourism sector. Indirect impacts of tourism through selling products or providing services has also been found to be limited. On the whole, the linkage of tourism with local economy is weak. A major effort needs to be made to develop and integrate the farming economy with tourism through appropriate economic and other policies.

DISPLACEMENT OF LOCAL PEOPLE

Tourism creates new employment opportunities in the host area and hence influences migration pattern in two principal directions: it helps the community to retain members who would otherwise migrate away, particularly unemployed or underemployed youths in economically marginal areas such as islands or mountains; but it also attracts outsiders who are searching for work or economic opportunity and who often come from other branches of the economy, particularly agriculture (de Kadt, 1979:35–36, 43). In primitive and isolated areas, arrival of too many visitors can even cause local people to leave their settlements and move to new areas where they can remain undisturbed (Archer and Cooper, 1997:81).

As Sauraha became very popular for tourism, many people are attracted to run a hotel and to take interest in buying land. Consequently, the land has become quite expensive. For example, in 1978 a *bigha* (0.67 ha) of land in Sauraha used to cost a meager NRs 4000 whereas in 2000 the same land costs 7 million rupees. Since the land was in demand and the price was high, the Tharus sold their land for financial reasons as well as attraction for large sum of money. The outsiders and the non-Tharus used the land as diamond and the Tharus misused the money as iron. In this context Muller-Boker (1999:83) shows the differences between the nature of Pahariyas and the Tharus. In this regard the author writes, 'they (Tharus) are convinced that the Pahariyas can do everything better and more energetically'. Over and over again I heard such utterances as ' We only know how to sell land, not how to buy it ...' It is said that the Tharus by tradition are extravagant in nature. Therefore, they spent money only on alcohol. As a result, many Tharus lost their homes and land. But, it does not mean that there are no Tharus at all in Sauraha. Nowadays a large portion of the Tharu habitation has been replaced by the non-Tharu groups. This reveals that the non-Tharus are getting direct benefit from tourism and Sauraha is becoming more a village of heterogeneous groups. In this regard, the report of KMTNC also shows that due to concentration and continuous flow of tourism industry in Sauraha, the land price of Sauraha has been increasing. The increase in land price is encouraging the Tharus to sell their land. The result of this is that the Tharus are being dislodged. This could be harmful to the tourist industry, as they and their culture is one of the main attraction for the tourists. Displacement of people from their ancestral lands through market mechanisms is something of a global concern related with the protection of indigenous cultures and livelihoods (KMTNC, 1996:6–9).

CULTURAL EFFECTS OF TOURISM

Tourists not only bring money to region, they also carry along with them a strong and visible life-style. Their dress, food habits and merry-making style all bring some newness and uniqueness to the area of their visit. By nature, human adopts new things or manners in which they feel comfortable. Sometimes, new habits are acquired from strangers just to get new taste.

Tourism represents a form of the process of social modernisation which can be interpreted as diffusion or as a form of social change because the structure and function of the social system can be modified through the invention, expansion , and adoption of new ideas, values, norms, behavioral patterns etc. External factors are usually the main force driving cultural change, renewal, and innovation. Within a society the process of passing on a culture implies conservation and continuity, while the expansion of a culture into other societies—the intercultural process—brings cultural change and discontinuity (Larkey, 1994).

As in other areas of impact, there is some debate over the nature and direction of the consequences of tourism for culture, but the dominant perspective is that it is harmful. Turner and Ash (1975) typified this perspective: The tourists' superior economic wealth rapidly erodes the sensuous and aesthetic wealth of cultures that have developed in isolation from the western world. Tourism of the present has already begun the work of obliterating cultures. A limited number of studies stress the positive effects of tourism on culture. 'If support for conservation is regarded as a desirable cultural trait, then the comments can be brought to work together to mutual benefit. Tourism and conservation are interdependent and both stand to gain from close and effective collaboration'. Thus, tourism can be viewed as a source of or remedy for problems. Both perspectives are examined below. The positive effects of tourism on culture through the promotion of intercultural communication is presented first and then the numerous other effects of tourism on culture are examined.

The Tharus consider the tourists rich and educated. They take different kind of food, wear neat and clean clothes and possess a lot of articles and instruments with them. They are good people and show much affection to the poor people. Their language and culture are better than their culture and language. They want to live in a clean environment. This reveals that the weaker hosts always appreciate the stronger guests and show a positive attitude towards them. Wolf (1982), who shifted the focus on how traditional societies have been drawn into these exploitative relationships. The relevance of dependency (Wallerstein, 1974) theory to the study of international tourism is clear: the idea of core regions exploiting peripheral areas is also applicable to many instances of domestic tourism. In line with this perspective, Schneider, et al. (1972) refer to tourism in parts of southern Europe as an example of modernisation without the corresponding economic development. However, there are big hotels and rich tourists on one side and indigenous people with their primitive mode of life represented by small shelters and big families having many children on the other side.

The Tharu boys who come from the same locality are seen quite inactive. The etic version is that they are imitating western lifestyle, high living-standard and spending money in beer and buying western cigarettes and clothes which is actually not good for their family and society. While supporting this view, one informant expressed that one of the native naturalists used to go home in the evening with indulging and insisted his traditional wife to perform western dance for making fun. The wife had never seen the western dance. According to the informants, imitating is not bad if it has positive results, but imitating something that is beyond one's means is not good at all. It has diverse effects on society as well as on individuals. The youth is indulging in what they cannot afford. They are suffering from inferiority complex, thinking that all foreign is good and superior, while they are inferior. The outsiders are spoiling their life because of taking hashes, drugs and drinks. Besides transforming from demonstration effect, the youngsters are also seen appreciating the total behavioral aspects of the foreigners which is known as xenocentrism (Warner et al., 1976: 271–274). Xenocentrism is the belief that what is foreign is best, that one's own lifestyle, products or ideas are inferior to those of others. Xenocentrism may focus on a product, an idea or a lifestyle. Regardless of the focus, it is assumed that native techniques and concepts are inferior. The opposite of ethnocentrism is xenocentrism (Eshleman and Cashion, 1983:95–96).

Many local traditions and habits have come under the influence of tourists in Sauraha. Influence of old customs and traditions has diminished in many areas. This is more common among both the Tharu and non-Tharu boys and girls, restaurant employees and naturalists of Shauraha who come in direct contact with the tourists. They have started wearing modern dresses and many of them speak good English. They crave to go to the west and to work there through establishing marital relation with the tourist girls. No Tharus of proper Sauraha and Odra villages have married any foreigner nor have they visited the western country. Similarly, no evidence has been found that the native girls have tried to get married with the tourist boys. Because of language problem, they cannot propose any thing with the tourists. Recently, a Tharu boy of Bachhauli got married with an Australian lady and went to Australia along with his wife.

In Chitwan, people believe in *paret* as one of the dangerous ghost that reside in wind. In order to drive this spirit away the elephant drivers offer worship on the bank of a river in Ashad (July). They also worship Lord Ganesh. According to their belief, the elephant is sometimes lost inside the forest and some elephant might become mad and run away. Therefore, for not having such incidence, they worship the forest deity known as *ban sapti*. The Tharus of Chitwan face a problem of not finding their oxen which they have lost in the forest. To find them the Tharus worship the same deity. They have another river goddess known as *jahar mai* which is also worshipped in the same month. The purpose of offering puja (sacred performance) to their goddess is not to have soil erosion from heavy flood. Every day there is elephant ride in the jungle which means the elephant drivers are closely associated with the tourists. But, they have not left their tradition. Belief system makes people more stronger. Still tourism has not affected the belief system of the elephant drivers.

The user group member and local community of Baghmara feel happy when they see tourists visiting their area. They had never expected that the tourists would multiply to such a big number. But contrary to this, they also voiced their opinion that they don't prefer the tourists' customs and values to some extent and are even scared that the young generation are getting trapped in it day by day. They are very worried with the drug problem as they feel that the tourists are the ones who introduce it to their village (Beun and Lamichhane, 1999:27).

While talking to the community members, they expressed that the tourists in many ways have influenced the Tharu community. Their culture has modified to some extent in their ways of dressing and living standards. Young people do not prefer hardships like farming. But Mina gaun, a village in ward No. 4 of Baghmara Community Forest, is the only one not influenced by tourists. The village committee has felt the need for preservation of tradition and culture and is planning in this regard (*ibid*). The chairman of Hotel Association of Sauraha remarks both the positive and negative aspects of tourism in Sauraha. According to Beun and Lamichhane (*ibid*, 29), the impacts are as follows: Economic level of the village has improved; Level of education among both men and women has increased; Health centre has been improved with better equipment; Sk ll development training for women is provided so that they can be financially independent. In the context of negative aspects, they write, culture is vanishing slowly among the youngsters by imitating the ways of tourists; Use of drug intake has increased compared to before (*ibid*).

According to Muller-Boker (1999:55), 'Shoestring tourism, on the other hand, concentrated in the area around Sauraha, has brought massive change in the socioeconomic structures of the region and given rise to appreciable excesses'.

But, while writing about the negative impact of tourism, she further shows that mostly those who are involved in tourism voice criticism. It was claimed that trouble and unrest had arisen, everyone was supposed to be fighting. It was said that hard drugs had been introduced to Sauraha and were not only consumed by foreigners, and that the encounter with tourists, especially with the female ones, goes to the young men's head. On the whole . . ., albeit showing some astonishment at tourist behavior (Muller-Boker, 2000:112).

But, no evidence of taking drugs by the natives and the tourists was found at the time of field work in 1993. However, the researcher was informed that a very few tourists want to smoke hashes during their jungle walk. In course of discussion it was found that the outsiders try to provide these things to the tourists for the purpose of earning money soon. Those people who look like junkie may take hashes and also offer to the tourists to maintain good relations with them. According to the local informants, some people by supplying girls and drugs develop good relations with the tourists. For this favour later on the tourist may invite him to visit his/her country. However, the etic version shows that there is conflict between the insiders and outsiders in the tourist destination. The insiders always hesitate to follow the activities conducive to adverse effects in tourism and on the tourists. Although some guides are spoiling their life by changing their habits as a result of the influence of some fnatic tourists, majority of them are very happy with this industry because it directly benefits their profession and economic prosperity.

The nature, habits, beliefs and traditions of the youngsters are also undergoing changes owing to the influences of the tourism industry. Their life is going to be more sophisticated, easy and fast. This reveals that the youngsters who are involved in tourism seem to be changed as temporocentrists. Temporocentrism is the belief that one's own time is more important than the past or future. This kind of example can be cited only among the individuals who have come to Sauraha far from their birth places. The young boys do not seem to be worried about their family members.

People sometimes talk about the young boys who

actually would not spoil their life, they are spoiling and who were in a position to spoil their life they have improved considerably. In Sauraha, when five or six friends meet together, they spend their evening time in the restaurants. They talk about tourists, take liquor and quarrel with each other. The tips which they get from the tourists are spent in the restaurants. The informants expressed that they walk inside the jungle along with the tourists for 3–4 h and get tired. Therefore, they go to the restaurants to drink and relax. Although they quarrel they do not have enmity with each other for a long time. The reason is that they have to work together within the limited area of the National Park. The natives, locals (the non-Tharu group of the area) and outsiders are all in a process of transformation. But it cannot be said that tourism is the only force that has brought transformation in the Tharu Community. All other forces are also equally responsible in bringing changes there. People work for survival, not for the betterment of their family or society.

These days the Osho Camp has become another important attraction centre for the local people. Those who regularly visit this centre have to change their dresses. The identity markers of the regular visitors are red dress and Osho bead. It is said that the purpose of visiting this centre is for meditation. The informants reported that more than 70 individuals of Sauraha periphery had already got membership from the center in 1999. Every morning, the Osho Camp provides vehicle to its members. Regarding their involvement at the center people comment in Sauraha. In this regard there are two groups with different opinions and arguments. One group argues that the involvement of youngsters at such type of center do not function to maintain their cultural identity. Again, this makes the individual more temporocentrist. After entering into the center, the individuals begin to show their free lifestyle instead of following their traditional norms, values, ethos and moral. Another group of school argues that this type of entry makes an individual more disciplined. From the viewpoint of tourism, Sauraha requires the disciplinary forces for the betterment of tourism. This will also function to keep Sauraha always a peaceful destination. Otherwise, Sauraha could be disturbed due to the deindividuation. Whatever the argument is, the Osho Camp has also become an agent of change in the studied area. In 2001 it was found that almost all the youths of Sauraha stopped visiting the Camp. The visitors felt that the act of spending 2 h for meditation further motivated them to relax for another couple of hours at home. People felt disturbed at their work in the field of tourism. If they could not work they would not get food. Therefore, they have left visiting the Camp. This also reveals that there is always a conflict between spiritualism and materialism.

In Chitwan, the Tharus first came into contact with the hill migrants such as Brahmins, Chhetris, Tamangs, Darais, Botes, Kumals, Gurungs and other government officials and then with the tourists. This is the place where three cultures (the Tharu culture, hill culture and the tourist culture) meet together. The Tharus developed man-to-man relationship in the urban area and became familiar with Indian and Nepali movies, aeroplane, motor-car, radio, television, modern education, modern agricultural tools, computer, internet, e-mail, fax and telephone. The Tharus' house is often small in size. By tradition, they used to live in extended family. There is a great significance of the male progenies. Therefore, a married woman would continue to bear children until the birth of a male child. This is one of the main reasons of having big families in the Tharu community. Nowadays majority of them have nuclear family. Out of 45 households, only 2 households have big family. One family comprises maximum 32 members who were sharing the same kitchen. The nuclear family system is an influence among them which has crept in from the hill migrants. Decoration of the exterior wall on the sides of the main door is found in Padampur village only. This elucidates that the Tharus of Sauraha are gradually leaving this tradition. The door-walls are decorated by rice-flour. This is done by the women on the day of *soharai* (one of the most important festivals of the Tharus of Chitwan observed in November). The housing design is also transforming in Sauraha. The main village of Sauraha is already electrified.

For Tharus in Chitwan, the Brahmins and their values represent the best available model for surviving and succeeding in a society where relationships both with other people and with things is mediated by cash. The Brahmin in this respect acts as a model not for sanskritisation but for modernisation, because, as far as the Tharu is concerned, he represents a successful adaptation to the changes in the economic order (Guneratne, 1999:172).

Traditional clothing for women consists of a short white skirt and a white shawl or length of cloth which is tucked into the waist at front and thrown over one shoulder to cover the breast. A short, dark blue or black bodice, either sleeveless or with short sleeves, is also worn at times. Because of recent influences, younger women now tend to wear saris. Very young girls today wear Weatern-style short skirts or pants, sometimes with a top, as other Nepali girls do. The women's clean, well combed hair is usually tied in a distinctive knot at the back of the head.

Jewellery traditionally consisted of *tharya*, heavy bracelets worn above the elbows on both arms, and a horseshoe-like neckband called a hansuli made of silver or an alloy; tharya and hansuli are not often seen nowadays. Decorative silver rings are also worn in noses and ears.

The traditional dress has been totally abandoned by the people of Sauraha. The women have almost left wearing their traditional ornaments. This is an influence of the Pahadi (hill) people and Indian movies. In Sauraha, the young Tharu boys are seen in clean, colorful, modern and wildlife dress. The women are seen wearing Chitwan National Park vest, frock, maxi, nightie or gown and other *pahadi* (hill) costume. The children are seen in school dress. Wearing traditional dress is supposed to be kind of inferior. Similarly the Tharus who are involved in tourism profession do not want to speak their language and also hesitate to discuss their traditional way of life. The reason is that they feel backward and inferior to others. There is much inferiority complex on one side and upward mobility is gradually increasing among them on the other side. This reveals that there is an increasing identity crises in the Tharu community. Internally they feel that they have become backward because of their own culture. But it cannot be said why they have taken their culture as curse? They refrain from being identified as 'Tharus'– rather they prefer to be addressed by their surname 'Chaudhary'.

Only the old women have their lower legs and occasionally their arms tattooed, often with peacock designs. Mainly for decoration, these tattoos are usually done before marriage. Tattooing was a must for women till recently but nowadays they do not want to have tattoo marks in order to preserve the beauty of their body. Earlier there was a belief that without tattoos marks, they would not be reincarnated. But now the young girls hold the opinion that if they go for tattoo, their skin would turn ugly. This feeling was created due to the impact of tourism, hill people, modern education, urban environment and movies. Whenever they get money they go to see a movie either to Tandi Bazaar or Narayanghat. They are crazy for movies. As regards their food habit, in the past the Tharus used to devote their entire day in ploughing and leveling the soil. At that time, they used to take food three or four times a day, but nowadays they have no work and also no food, which means they take only two meals a day only. This is also a influence of the hill people. In the same manner their kitchen utensils have also changed.

In agricultural work they learnt knitting and weeding of paddy and maize from the hill migrants. These days the artifacts can be rarely seen at the Tharu houses. The housing design, room structure and kitchen utensils have also changed in Tharu villages. The household materials have been replaced by the modern materials. The village of Sauraha is already electrified. If necessary they can use telephone, computer and are e-mail and internet. But, this is not possible for the Tharus who live in the interior villages. Life is going to be sophisticated in Sauraha. In one talk, the non-native entrepreneur of Sauraha expressed that there is no reason for visiting Kathmandu because every thing is available in Sauraha.

Twice a year, the people of Sauraha perform two rituals in their village shrine called *baramthan*. They are *esaribarna* and *leuribarna*. These rituals are observed in July and October respectively. In the past, people had lot of work throughout the year. Therefore, they needed relaxation and they did so. Since they do not have to work in the fields these days, they celebrate only for a day. This rite is performed by the village priest called *gurau*. In the past, until the ritual is not over, the women were not permitted to drink water from the well. Nowadays, there is a water tap everywhere and they do not adhere to this rule. While writing about the cultural effects of tourism in the Tharu community of Sauraha, Muller-Boker focuses (2000:112) on 'the so called *barna*' and 'tharu stick dance' in the context of change. People supplied their oxen for transporting tourists even on the day of *barna*, which was totally prohibited before, and dance became a commodity. People earn money from both activities. Therefore, the writer considers it as a positive change. Mishra and Jefferies (1991:131–132) write, 'in Sauraha this tradition had almost disappeared because of tourism and outside influences'.

Deeply rooted in the Tharus' traditional way of life is the institution of the *gurau*, who functions as a mediator between the 'supernatural' and the real world (Muller-Boker, 1999:74). These days the role of the village priest or the faith-healer, *gurau*, is gradually declining in Sauraha. Earlier the faith-healer used to perform *dewai* worship. The purpose of performing this ritual was to ward off any kind of disease from the children. But, these days nothing is heard about this ritual. People had strong belief in witchcraft. The witchcraft was controlled by *gurau* in the past. Now-a-days the youngsters do not even talk about witch. Their strong belief in the supernatural forces is gradually declining. No young boy wants to learn traditional method of healing from an old and experienced *gurau*. The young boys think that simply learning this method would not be useful in this modern world. The reason is they are influenced by the modern tourists, facilities of modern hospitals and modern education. Even they have started observing festivals on a small scale. The older generation regret and tell that earlier the money earned by them was used for fulfilling the needs of all the members of the family, but now, if the daughter or son's wife earns some money, it becomes her personal property. The concept of individualism is gradually increasing within the family members of the Tharus. The idea of collectivism is gradually decreasing. There is also a clash between the older and younger generations. Buying new clothes is one of the main activities of the youngsters. They are highly influenced by the modern lifestyle. Previously the bullock carts were the means of their transport. Now the people of younger generation use cycle and motorbike in and around the villages. Because of the flow of tourists in Sauraha, local people frequently get a chance to go to the market of Tandi. The hotel owners while driving jeep back and forth from Sauraha give lift to the Tharus or other local people. The Tharus make fun of this kind of lift. It is because traveling by jeep is more convenient than by a bullock cart. This reveals that they are in a process of urbanisation.

The older people informed that earlier when they were young, they used to sing and dance during marriage and death rites. The dances performed during the above-mentioned ceremonies is called *rasdhari*. Now, this tradition has been left out by the young boys and girls. In the past there was no system of giving dowry to the daughter. Now dowry is a must. Regarding this change, the informants express that the practice of giving dowry is not good for the poor people. Nowadays a Brahmin priest is hired to perform their marriage ceremony. This reveals that they are in a process of sanskritisation (Srinivas, 1965) and pahadisation (the process of becoming similar to the hill migrants).

Among the festivals, *fagui* (festival of colors), *jitiya* (fasting ceremony) and *soharai* are very popular in the Tharu community of Chitwan. *Fagui* is observed by the males whereas *jitiya* is observed by the females. According to the tradition, the whole household is compelled to participate in these ceremonies. But, due to the changed context, the rate of participation in these festivals is very low. Owing to their involvement in tourism, many do not participate in this program and pay NRs. 10 as fine, and this is a very easy method of escaping from these traditional gatherings. In 1992 and 1998, the Tharu festivals were organised at Sauraha on the inspiration of the Ministry of Tourism and Tharu Welfare Committee respectively. In both festivals, the Tharus of different parts of Terai (including Chitwan) exhibited their local dances for 2–3 days. Since then the Tharus of Sauraha are participating in all their festivals and ceremonies with great enthusiasm. But it does not mean that the culture has been revitalised in Sauraha.

Almost the material culture of Sauraha is already replaced by the modern materials. These days there cannot be seen any of the following traditional tools and artifacts around Sauraha: *henga, pala, tabada, byawa, dhariya, koin, jhaara, khenhari, perngo, eisgina, jhajha, jhopata, duhuri, dibari, tarkani, jhoki, dhakiya, edhiya, gonari, khithira, hadhi, ghaila, dhakana, ghelwari, chipana, tap, chachra, bharahi, kargaha, khanti, swela, bhenga, chalani, suppa, southi, gohara, shable, sarngi, khurbudiya, thakari, pedaha, damphu, chatiya, khurpa, khurpi, topcar chatiea, machiya, doxy, khatiya, thathara, patchis, bewa, pantopani* (basket), *tokari, nwon daheni, theki* (milk churning material), *jant* (grinding stone), *sabai ki birni botai* (plaiting grass ready for storing), *gonari bina* (mat), *patuha* (*pataha* grass), *khadahi* (a kind of grass), *hengoe* (field flattener), *pitina* (clothes bitting material), *kharahar* (broom which is used only at the courtyard), *deli* (fishing pot), *binda* (ring disk which is placed on the head), *jhonki* (where utensils are placed), *chingani othara* (chicken house), *bagani* (broom which is used only inside the room), *chokari* (mat), *garjanto* (mouse killing trap), *koini* (fish trap), *danra* (basket which is used for keeping puffed rice or bitten rice), *chhatiya* (umbrella), *kapatur othara* (pigeon's house), *bangi* (basket where the grains are stored), *diuwa* (burning lamp), *basila* (wood cutting tool), *bijita* (sitting mat), *bhala* (wooden bow), *jaal* (fish net), *byana* (fan), *tuma* (limestone keeping bag), *kharau* (sandal), *jhora* (fish keeping bag), *parango* (dried fish keeping bag), *dharni* (meat, grains measuring unit), *khanti* (digging material), *silota* (spices grinding tool), *byawna* (fish material), *pala rhyanga* (field leveler), *tangi* (axe), *har* (plough material), *bahinga* (stick), *dhewar* (fish net), *suila* (stick), *thagiya* (fishing material), *kolahu* (wooden material which produces cooking oil from mustard), *usukuna* (dispersed rice collector), *dhenki* (rice husking tool), *topi* (traditional hat), *dirwata* (lamp placing spot), *toki* (lamp). All these materials are made of materials available in the forest and locally available materials. All these materials have been replaced by the modern materials.

STAGED AUTHENTICITY

Vallee (1987) maintained that 'Authenticity is a desired and actively pursued experience by tourists which is perceived to reflect or give access to the true and unadulterated nature of everyday life in the destination'. According to Getz (1997:315), 'Authenticity means genuine, unadulterated or "the real thing." For Boorstin (1964:103) attractions are 'of little significance to the inward life of a people, but wonderfully saleable as tourist commodity', for MacCannell they are highly significant social symbols. Boorstin takes it for granted that 'attractions' are inauthentic; he states that 'Tourist attractions serve their purpose best when they are pseudo-events', since in his view tourists seek illusions. MacCannell's tourist, however, is concerned with the authenticity of the attractions. The quest for authenticity, indeed, rather than the search for contrived illusions, is said to be the fundamental motivation of modern tourists. Since, modern man is alienated from his own inauthentic and shallow world, he seeks authenticity elsewhere in other times and other places (MacCannell, 1976:3). He has used the term 'backstage' to describe the physical setting in which a visitor could observe, meet or share something authentic. In order to prove his concept, MacCannell (*ibid*) writes, 'no one can participate in his own life, he can only participate in the lives of others'. Moreover reactions to MacCannell's approach were less critical than that to Boorstin's (Cohen, 1988: Nash, 1996:141–142). Cohen (1979) and Pearce (1982) have added to the debate by arguing that visitor satisfaction will depend not only on the nature of the event (whether or not it is authentic) but also on the visitor's perception of whether or not authenticity exists and their need for authentic experiences. For example, one visitor will want a festival to be an authentic culture, finds a highly commercialised tourist-oriented event, another visitor will not care and still others will not know the difference. Authenticity can be considered as a part of the event product, because it is something that can motivate certain tourists, and it is a benefit that can at least partially be controlled by organisers (Getz, 1997:316).

Authenticity is categorised into three types:

(i) Perceived authenticity,
(ii) Original authenticity and
(iii) Created authenticity.

In perceived authenticity, the tourists before their departure are subject to a range of images of the destination. Many are market oriented, others are unbiased documentary accounts of the region to be visited. The original authenticity is represented by the natural and man-made features which attract visitors to the destination region. If the original authenticity has been changed due to development or environmental damage then it is replaced by created authenticity (Jackson, 1989:104–105).

It is held that while buying the destinations the tourists also buy the culture of the host society. In Sauraha the buyers delightfully enjoy the Tharu cultural program which is popularly known as Tharu stick dance. This dance is performed generally in the evening either at individual lodges or Culture House. Till before 1998, there was a tradition of performing Tharu stick dance at different lodges of Sauraha. This dance is very popular not only in Sauraha but also at the resorts inside the National Park. About 24–30 people of Padampur-Bankattha (located inside National Park) had great monopoly in this business till before their translocation at Sagun Tole. The group charged Rs. 400 for one program at a hotel in 1993 and now they charge NRs. 800. The program lasts for an hour. In this program, the

Tharus offer four/five varieties of programs to the tourists. The dancers do not get the money directly from the hotels. The dancers come to the hotels on bicycles along with their musical instrument and dress. After reaching the hotel, they change their dress and prepare an altar. Then they start the performance of the dance.

From 1998 onward, after the translocation of the Tharus of Bankattha, two groups from Patna and Dorangi villages have started giving culture programs in Sauraha. Since the program was introduced at Culture House in 1998, majority of the guides and hotel managers feel it convenient to take their individual guests at the Centre charging NRs. 75 each. Recently one more Culture House has been constructed and it shows varieties of dance program representing the different ethnic groups of Nepal. Those who individually sell the program, they might get rake-off from the manager of Culture House. In the view of guides, this is a positive impact of tourism because the local people have now got a chance to sell their culture to their guests.

As far as the Tharu culture program in concerned, among the different items of dances, the first item is locally called *bhajeti* in which they play with large sticks. The second item is known as *damphu* which is played on the occasion of *fagui* festival in February. The third item is known as *thekara*. This is also played on the same occasion. The fourth item is known as *jhili* and in it they can sing any kind of song in course of their dance. In this item, the tourists are also invited to dance along with the dancers. The first item is not an originally developed dance of this community. It has been borrowed from outside. This can be said that the Tharu stick dance program is an invented tradition. According to Hobsbawn and Ranger (1997:1), the term 'invented tradition' includes both 'traditions' actually invented, constructed and formally instituted and those emerging in a less easily traceable manner within a brief and desirable period—a matter of a few years perhaps—and establishing with great rapidity. Now, everywhere in the Tharu habitat, the stick dance has been institutionalised as one of their original cultural forces.

The item of *damphu* is performed only by those people who have got a drum. In the village, this is traditionally performed by the older people because the young boys do not have this instrument during this function. Therefore, the young boys would dance along with their small sticks. On this occasion, the older people dance and drink. Though the children also take part in this dance, they do not drink. The involvement of children in this dance program is called *thekara*. Previously people used to perform this ritual dance from the day of waxing moon to the time of full moon but now they have shortened this ritual program to 2–3 days only and it has become more commercialised now. The women do not perform this dance except on the day of *jitiya* festival. The third item, *jhili* is performed only at the time of *hari kirtan,* in which mostly the devotional songs are sung by the people of Sauraha. Some groups perform peacock dance too.

The package tourists do not find time to know the host people in a better way. Therefore, they want to be familiar with the host people only through staged program. Such kind of cultural activities performed on stage are called 'front region of the destination which helps to protect the "back region", resident's homes and areas where local life continues' (MacCannell, 1973). One of the problems of 'alternative tourism' is that the tourists are encouraged to penetrate this 'back region' (Archer and Cooper, 1997:81). Upon inquiry in different hotels at the time of field work, it was found that no guide was able to explain the details about the culture of Tharus and the significance of the cultural programme.In those places people do not realise that tourism is a service-oriented industry. In the context of change in the dancing programmes, the Tharus nowadays prefer to sing Indian and Nepalese film songs than their traditional songs. This is the influences of the movies. The tourists generally do not understand the meaning of the songs and dances. However, they participate in the last item of dance, to make fun and enjoy the events. The poor briefing of the guides make the tourists more confused. Since the tourists are confused and unable to understand, they laugh and are amused by these programmes. The main reason for this is that the guides are mostly given training only on nature not on culture. It was found that no briefing was given about the cultural program at Culture House.

ALLEGED THEFTS

It was reported that the main problems in Bachhauli VDC is theft, threatening and suicide. Ethnically people who are involved in crime belong to the non-Tharu group. Annually 4–5 suicides occur due to madness and divorce. It is not clear whether those incidents occur due to the impact of tourism. There has been a rise in criminal activities since tourism flourished. There are many cases of theft, particularly in Sauraha where a large number of tourist stay and enjoy the cultural program in the evening. These programs are often an hour long, and it is during this period that the culprits take advantage of this situation and steal tourists' belongings and money from those hotels and lodges. This incident has made the staff more cautious in the evening particularly at the time of the cultural program. Although the thieves were native people, they did not hail from Sauraha. The tourists are always considered to be rich because they move with a lot of articles with them.

EROTIC PLEASURE

The relationship or inequality between host and guest is played out at an intimate level in the co-occurrence of prostitution and tourism in many parts of the world. Anthropologists have written in particular about sex tourism in Southeast Asia (Cohen, 1982). Apart from prostitution, sexual relations between hosts and guests often reflect the differences in power between the host and sending countries.

Though prostitution is not institutionalised in Sauraha, the informants reported that very few tourists, particularly FIT those staying for 4/5 days, take interest and are involved with the local girls. In course of discussion, few informants showed their negative attitude towards prostitute girls because of their involvement with the tourist. While asking about the informants' involvement with these kinds of girls, it was expressed that they get a lot of opportunity to meet with the tourist girls who, because of their white complexion, look more beautiful than the local ones. There comes again *xenocentrism.* The guide's main intention remains to please the tourists to get more tips, and finally to get a chance to visit abroad. According to them, the tourist girls themselves propose to indulge men in amorous pleasure. Therefore, visiting brothels house is of no use because they cannot get any benefit from there. It was also reported that a few guides want to appease the tourists by providing such type of girls with a view to get more tips from him. One informant reported that so and so managed one girl to a tourist and the tourist became quite happy with this. Later on, he sent US $ 3000 to his guide from his home. Although such type of examples can be found in this area, the young boys who have come from outside, either visit prostitutes or gamble or drink. Another information was that the guides are greatly liked by those girls because of their regular contact with them. Another reason for this is that the guides can spend more money in the activity. Awareness of AIDS among girls and boys has brought down their involvement in sex activities. Most of the girls are now married and the boys have restrained themselves from these activities. It is not known whether the girls working in the sex industry had benefitted economically as some guides have reported that they are paid less than promised. For example, a girl is hired by promise of a thousand rupees and is paid only hundred rupees. This study shows that prostitution is not directly related or influenced from the tourists but the local workers involved in the industry of tourism. Here the term local workers means people who work in tourism and they are quite far away from the family. The native people do not involve themselves in such activities because they are under the bondage of the relatives and family. Another reason for prostitution is the low economy of the local people. Prostitution has not been openly accepted by the Nepalese society.

TOURISM AND ETHNICITY

Ethnicity is one of the most important forms of intra-cultural variation studied by anthropologists. In actual use, ethnicity occupies the conceptual space between biogenetic ideas of race and sociogenetic ideas of culture. Ethnic attractions always stress the importance of emerging self-consciousness and self-determination of the ethnic minority. The focus is on a type of tourism in which exotic cultures figure as key attractions: where the tourists go to see folk costumes in daily use, shop for folk handicrafts in authentic bazaars, stay on the alert for a typical form of nose, lips, breast etc., learn some local norms for comportment, and perhaps learn some of the language (MacCannell, 1984:377). MacCannell has also described two types of ethnicity: constructed ethnicity and reconstructed ethnicity. Constructed ethnicity is only a conceptual springboard to a more complex phenomenon. The term constructed ethnicity is used to refer to efforts such as means and to the various ethnic identities which emerged via opposition and assimilation during the colonial phase of Western history and in the new 'internal colonies'.

The term reconstructed ethnicity is used here to refer to the kinds of ethnic identities which have emerged in response to pressures from tourism. The economic structure of ethnic tourism is such that most of the money involved does not change hands at the site. Most of the money is spent on luggage, cameras, clothing, air plane tickets, tour bus rides etc. before and after the actual visit. Even though the ethnic attraction may be the entire reason for making the trip, while at the town itself, tourists often spend nothing at all, or they make whimsical purchases of souvenirs, or buy a beer or an ice cream cone or make a dollar donation to a local restoration project. Ethnic reconstructions for tourists in particular inject new complexities into the relationship of social and economic values. While the attention of tourists may provide some intangible 'payoffs' in the form of flattery, it is difficult to find concrete benefits in this type of ethnic tourism for the people whose life is the attraction (*ibid*, 386). Reconstructed ethnicity is the maintenance and preservation of ethnic forms for the entertainment of ethnically different others. Reconstructed ethnicity is fully dependent on the earlier stages in the construction of ethnicity. But it represents an end to the dialogue, a final freezing of ethnic imagery which is both artificial and deterministic. The new reconstructed ethnic forms are produced once almost all the groups in the world are located in a global network of interactions and they begin to use their former colorful ways both as commodities to be bought and sold and as rhetorical weaponry in their dealings with one another. Suddenly, it is not just ethnicity anymore, but it is understood as rhetoric, as symbolic expression with a purpose or a use value in a large system. It is high time to develop reconstructed ethnicity in the neighboring villages of Sauraha for sustainable tourism.

According to Hotel and Community Development Committee, as it was recorded in August 1997, the number of registered hotels (including restaurants) was 48. Out of 48, there were 20 hotels run by the Brahmins (41.66%), 14 by the Newars (29.1%), 5 by the Chhetris(10.4%), 5 by the Tharus (10.4%), 1 by the Magar (2.08%), 1 by the Limbu (2.08%) and 2 by unknown groups (4.1%). While observing jeep drivers' ethnicity, there were only 7 Tharus involved in the jeep driving occupation. The remaining other drivers belonged to the non-Tharu groups. Majority of the Tharus were found to be involved only in canoe ride. In the context of guide ethnicity, it was noticed from the Guides Associations of Sauraha, that the number of renewed guides was 62. Out of 62, there are 32 Brahmins (61.29%), 9 Tharus (14.57%), 6 Chhetris (9.67%), 2 Botes (3.21%), 2 Kumals (3.21%), 1 Magar (1.61%), 1 Tailor (1.61%), 1 Gurung (1.61%), 1 Newar (1.61%) and 1 unknown (1.61%). There are not less than 200 personnel who take care of the elephants inside and outside the national park. Both the *maots* (elephant drivers) and *fanits* (elephant care takers) have got employment in the field of tourism. Ethnically, they belong to the Tharus of neighboring areas and distant areas of Chitwan. It does not mean that other ethnic guides are not involved in tourism in Sauraha. For example, there is an eminent blacksmith naturalist who is running his own Guide Office at the same place.

As far as the employees of lodges inside the park is concerned, some ethnic variations are found: lodge owners from Kathmandu, managers and few naturalists from Deharadun and Darjeeling, India, and few naturalists and other low paid staff from the locality—the Tharus.

During field work, it was observed that the guides were poorly interpreting the culture of the Tharus while performing the Tharu stick dance (cultural program) at various Camps. Realising the problem of this fact, Department of Tourism deputed the present researcher to provide a training program on cultural interpretation technique to the naturalists of Sauraha for a week in 1997. Altogether 78 participants (both professionals and non-professionals) came to register for this program. Out of which, there were 42 Brahmins (53.8%), 18 Tharus (25.0%), 6 Chhettris (7.6%), 4 Newars (5.8%), 3 Tamangs (3.33%), 2 Botes (2.5%), and 1 Blacksmith (1.28%). The above-mentioned data reveals that the Tharus were on the front and the Brahmins and Newars on back before the introduction of tourism in Sauraha. Now the scenario is opposite. The front–back dichotomy (Goffman, 1959) shows that the non-Tharus captured (not in negative) both the sides of road in Sauraha and behind it were the Tharus. But, it does not mean that the Tharus' land was confiscated by the outsiders. In this context, the researcher feels it convenient to quote Guneratne's expression on ethnicity regarding the Tharus of Chitwan. As he writes, 'ethnicity is the cultural expression of the political economic fact: the confrontation between groups over resources of same kind. When the Tharus believe that some culturally defined group not the rich but the Brahmins benefit disproportionately or on unfairly in the allocation of resources, then ethnicity is likely to come into play as a "mask of confrontation" (Guneratne, 1998:770). But, there does not seem any kind of confrontation between the two groups. Ethnic harmony is still found Sauraha.

VILLAGE TOUR

Village tour is made by bullock cart or on foot. The tour covers most of the villages of Bachhauli VDC and Patna, Marchauli and Dhindauli of Padampur VDC. In Sauraha complex there are two villages, Sauraha proper has 20 Tharu households (out of 70 houses and few hotels) and Odra village has 25; the distances of the two villages is less than a kilometer. This shows that these two villages are centrally located within the tourist destination. Sauraha is nucleus whereas Odra is compact. Therefore, these villages function as the centre of tourist attraction. Though the tourists visit different villages, they are not well informed about the local people and their culture. Many tourists regretted that they could not get proper information about the people and their culture during their stay in Sauraha. The guides want to appease the tourists only by showing wildlife; they often abstain from explaining the culture and tradition of the native people. For the development of the cultural/ethnic tourism, cultural interpretation is also equally important. The guide should be well trained in briefing the native's culture. Then only the tourists will come to know the native's values which finally works to preserve and revitalise the culture.

There is a motorable road which links the two villages (Sauraha and Odra) and provides easy mobility to the tourists. Each and every moment the guests move around these two villages in course of their visit to the National Park. While visiting those villages, the tourists not only enjoy the lifestyle of the villagers but they also make fun by observing the movement of cattle, dog, ducks, chicken, sheep and goat. On both sides of the road, many signboards of hotels, guide offices, restaurants including menu boards, trekking arrangement and bus–train information centers have been hung. In the evening one can see the tourists eating food on the roof of the restaurants. All the restaurants have electricity and modern music echoes in the evening.

The tourists while walking on the road see the local Tharu children playing with bare feet either on the roadside or in the courtyard of their houses. The adult members are found busy with work hard in their houses. Whenever they get leisure time, they sit, talk, eat and sleep. Both sides of the road are often dirty owing to the garbage, water bottles, toilet paper, cigarette, cheese-ball and plastic bags. From October to April the roads are dry and dusty, while during monsoons (June-September) they are slushy and wet. Tourist slogan, 'Come as a guest go as a friend' can be seen in various places, for example at the front wall of the houses. The hoteliers, restaurant workers, shop owners and the guides talk about the tourists' behavior and their business but the Tharus talk about their work for the next day.

In course of the village tour program, the guides as culture brokers take the tourists to Odra, Malpur, Badreni, Bachhauli, Sauraha and Dorangi villages inhabited by the Tharus, Gurungs, Tamangs, Botes, Danuwars, Magars, Dhobis, Bahun–Chhetris and Damais. Much depends on the guides about where the tourists will be taken in one of the above-mentioned villages. While having a village tour, the tourists feel very happy on seeing the people, their traditional lifestyle, houses, their way of dressing, children, activities and the environment of the area. Nunez (1989) describes culture brokers in the following terms: 'It is clear that in most situations a handful of people, on more economically or intellectually advantaged than their peers, appear to emerge as culture brokers. They learn the necessary second or third language; they change occupations from subsistence or salaried to entrepreneurial; they migrate to potential or developing resort areas, etc.; and if they are successful, they are emulated by the previously less daring'.

Some of the tourists visit the villages without the help of the guides. Such tourists take picture of the local people. In return, they give clothes, chocolate, pencil, money (Nepalese coin) etc. The groups handled by the guides do not provide such amenities to the local people on account of the directions of the guides. The local people sometimes compare between the tourists of the past and the present. Earlier many people used to get many things from the tourists.

While these days the tourists refrain from giving anything to the local people because they are afraid of bringing changes. Previously the tourists gave money to the local people to buy land, jeep etc. and to run hotel. They contributed money for the education of many children. Many of them took their guides to their countries also. Rabin Shrestha (pseudonym), a guide of Eden Guest House, purchased 8 *katha* of land with the money received from a French tourist. A blacksmith of Malpur got 1,00,000 Rs. to construct a lodge from the tourist. A man named Mohan of Padampur village is getting US $ 75 per month for his study in Kathmandu. More than 100 people of the Chitwan National Park area are getting regular help from the tourists who visited Sauraha in the past (based on the data of 1993). However, some of them who are getting this monetary help are misusing their money. They often indulge themselves consuming drinks, and in purchasing dresses of western style. In the long run they not only exhaust the money given to them by the tourists but also their parental property because of these habits

The above-mentioned relationship does not show the total interaction between the hosts and guests. The study shows that there is also a gap of cultural communication between the hosts and guests except the demonstration effect. The tourists just look at the local people, smile and think about them and return. The local people do not show any positive response to the observation of the tourists. It is because both of them have a language problem. Language barriers frequently increase the social distance between many tourists and hosts. The way of touring the village is a kind of phenomenal observation. In most cases it is a silent dialogue of the kind described by Martin Buber the philosopher—a communication by look, gesture and general manner of behavior (Swinglehurst, 1997:92). Besides this, the tourists of Sauraha seem quite busy in completing the itineraries given by the lodge owners. Therefore, they do not have much time to keep in close contact and visit people. Another reason for this gap is because the guides are unable to brief the tourist about the society and culture of the people. But, in some situation, '... bilingual tour guides gain a great deal of power from being able to control conversations between mono lingual guests and hosts' (Cohen, 1985). Many anthropologists, state policy and tourist brochures discourage the tourists to keep direct contact with the local residents (Graburn and Moore, 1994:239).

The villagers recall that the tourists of the past were quite nice and appreciated the local people. But, these days they are indifferent. Those who work in the kitchen and restaurants for them have no chance of getting anything from the tourists. However, the guides who work with them very often get good tips. In course of discussion with the villagers it was found that a young tailor of Sauraha got the opportunity to get education in Kathmandu with the financial help of a tourist. Later on the tourist bought some land for him in Sauraha and also took him to his country. The elephant drivers also, like the guides, get the tips from the tourists.

In the context of describing tourism as personal transition, MacCannell (1992:283–309), in his latest book, alludes to this issue in discussing tours of Westerners to places like the Sepik river in New Guinea, another region populated with people who often have been taken to be among the most primitive in the world. The tourists here have come mostly from Europe and represent what MacCannell refers to as a post-modern culture. The natives, whom many of these tourists take to be real primitives, actually are, according to MacCannell, 'ex-primitives' who already have acquired post-modern ways (but not, perhaps, as whole-heartedly as MacCannell implies). So, the two sides meet in a kind of never-never-land—the 'empty meeting grounds' of his title.

Generally, 'a mix of employers, employees, unemployed, professionals, academics, students and the multitude of other groupings can meet on common ground at a tourist destination' (Jackson, 1989:95). Sauraha is also not exceptional from those group of people—the insiders and outsiders respectively. While inquiring about the nationalities, some guides described that it is very difficult to generalise about which tourist is good or bad? Every tourist comes to this place with a different view. One group of guides informed that the German tourists are quite nice because they love them and have no complaint of any thing against them. The English tourists are all right. The Americans have always got a superiority complex. The Israeli tourists are disliked in Sauraha. The guides do not expect any kind of tips from the Indian tourists. Japanese tourists are also liked in Sauraha. Some guides unhesitatingly express that they have three/four girlfriends of so and so country. Some guides regretfully express that the female tourists are selfish. During their presence, the guides get a lot of assurance from them. But when they go back to their countries, they even do not write a single letter. In course of discussions the guides working in Sauraha categorised the whole tourists into two groups. Of the total tourists visiting Sauraha, 50% tourists like to see traditional culture and environment in the course of their visit to Sauraha. The changed attitude of the Tharus towards tourists and tourism is a kind of 'internal differentiation' as used by Young (1966). The term refers to the host community's capacity to process information types and experiences created by tourism. Internal differentiation effects are those internal changes brought about by the arrival of tourists. These changes include the development of new jobs and skills, the development of regional tourist system and the effects of the exchange of values and cultures between the host community and the visitor (Jackson, *op cit.*, 114). Regarding the behavior of guides, some of them expressed that they want to be junkie because the tourists like them to be so. This is an impact of the Pokhara lake side tourism and complex tourist activities of the Thamel area in Kathmandu.

The guide facility in every hotel should be improved by related training. There must be comprehensive training curriculum courses for employer with good knowledge in history, culture and ecology. A wildlife information center should be established which could give detailed information about animals, trees, shrubs, herbs as well as about natural building materials, traditional use of plants, herbal medicine and much more. As quality deteriorates, the tourism product is proved to be degraded, so there must be quality controls in hotel/lodges and the travel trade because undercutting prices below economy means loss of service quality provided to the tourists and this has an effect on marketability in RCNP (Sapkota, op. cit.).

Solid waste management and a dumping site belonging to most important problem in Sauraha. If the tourism sector is being developed intensively, the problems are even more increasing since usually tourist produce much more waste than inhabitants do. So it is obvious that a really well organised sanitation, a proper solid waste management and environment friendly dumping site are the most essential conditions for successful tourism development in the area (*ibid*).

ETHNIC ARTS AND SOUVENIRS

Souvenirs, derived from the Latin 'sub venire', 'to come to mind' are an important symbolic adjunct to the tourism industry, providing the tourist with something tangible to take home while simultaneously providing local employment in an arts and crafts industry (Smith, 1989:201).

Tourism has regenerated or revived indigenous arts in a number of cases studied by anthropologists. It is argued that sometimes customs and traditions coming to the brink of vanishing under the impact of industrialisation and urbanisation are revived due to tourism. Singh (1989) also finds such evidence in his survey of tourism impact on environment in Kullu valley in Himachal Pradesh in India. Dogan (1989) finds instances of tourism contributing to the development of pottery, basketry, jewelry and leather goods in Cyprus and Tunisia. In India as well government has supported fairs and festivals to boost cultural tourism (Dhar, 1993). Protection of historical buildings in England and India (Pearce, 1982; Dhar, 1993) has benefited from tourism (cited in Batta, 2000). While the productions of handicrafts is upheld as one of the best ways for groups without other industries to capitalise on their local culture, anthropologists have shown that the transformation of ethnic arts into tourist arts often can produce great changes in both the form and content of those arts.

Graburn has proposed a typology of the 'portable arts' for cross-sultural analysis:

(1) unctional fine arts, which have great contemporary cultural and social significance to the people themselves, comparable to Balineses offerings and temple carvings
(2) commercial fine arts, made for sale to a specialised audience of patrons or connoisseur, analogous to tapestries hung in Balinese places or ornamental carvings decorating the homes of the wealthy
(3) souvenir arts, made for sale to a wider audience, which in Bali include inexpensive carvings, paintings, masks, clothes, and jewelery and
(4) assimilated fine arts, including those attempts to copy or use the traditional arts of the outsiders by whom they are being influenced.

Graburn (1976) introduced the idea that art in contact with other cultures will diverge into two forms: one for outsiders (for trade, but also for presentation of an image) and one for insiders (maintaining ethnic identity and values). The phenomenon of selling less detailed art to outsiders while retaining the finest for insider consumption.

The form of art which is sold to the tourist is called airport art (Graburn, 1967) or fake art. Generally the size and shape of art objects become gradually smaller to which Smith has coined the term as trinket culture. The process of becoming smaller shape of the art is called trinket art (Smith, 1989).

There are two souvenir shops in Sauraha. Museum also sells some local products to the tourists. In response to the needs and buying patterns of tourists, the indigenous traditional art objects have been collected from different parts of Tharu habitat. Thus, the ethnic art has been commoditised in the tourist market of Sauraha. But, there is sold not only the Tharu art and craft but also sold the other mixed arts brought from different places. The Tharu's attractive materials are dresses, ornaments, buckets and baskets (made of forest materials). But, no outfit and ornaments are sold because these are already disappearing in the Tharu community as mentioned earlier. If those materials, those identity markers, are revived for tourism purpose, the natives would be highly benefitted from selling those products to the tourists. One can collect those materials from different Tharu sub-groups such as the Rana Tharus, Katharia Tharus, Deshauri Tharus, Dangaura Tharus, Deukhariha Tharus and Lampuchhuwa Tharus. One can install a different culture-based sovenir shop where the proposed materials can be exhibited through manequin. There is a great potential of running this kind of shop in Sauraha. This will not distroy the natives' culture. Rather it will help to revive the lost culture of the natives. At present, only the different size and form of buckets and baskets are available in Sauraha.

The most highly developed basket making tradition in Nepal is practiced by the Tharus, the oldest tribe in the Nepali Terai. Living deep in the jungle apart from their Hindu neighbors to the south and tribal groups in the hills, they have an endless supply not only of grasses for weaving but also peacock feathers, polished seeds and small freshwater mollusk shells for decorating the fringes of the finished baskets. Intricate designs in deep purple, green, red, and blue and black are woven in coil technique against a background of natural golden yellow. Bridegrooms holding pennants and riding on elephants , people holding hands in a circle and intricate flower designs decorate even the most utilitarian baskets for daily use. Baskets to be carried on the head in wedding processions are given a lacelike fringe of seeds and shells that jingle when carried. Baskets are woven so tightly that they can hold water. Baskets with tight-fitting tops for holding valuables have overlay designs woven into the edges representing flies and rat's teeth to ward off these common village foes. Several years of labour may be required to prepare the set of baskets to accompany the bride to her new house (Eckerd, 1979:12–18).

The Tharus were once completely self-sufficient, making everything they needed from natural products around them. Their skill lies in their ability to turn local grasses and canes into household items. To combat the heat, fans are made from fine grass stalks, lashed together with different coloured threads in a variety of patterns and edged with a frill of brightly-patterned cotton cloth. These fans are both decorative and practical. Wide conical baskets called *dauri* (in Chitwan) are made from the young, inner leaves of *Saccharum spoantaneum* These are coiled, then interwoven and decorated in various patterns with other grasses dyed cerise, green and yellow. They are used for holding grains and vegetables, for steaming rice and for storing clothing. The art of making *dauri* is being lost because the grasses for making them are difficult to find except within the Park, where collection is not permitted (Mishra and Jefferies,1991:138).

However, the outsider natives are encourage to make such type of materials on a larger scale. At least they have got a chance to sell their skill and they have been tapped by the souvenir sellers. This is a kind of revitalisation of traditional culture or cultural involution (McKean, 1989)—tourism inspired revivals of traditional aspects of culture.

Chapter Six

ALTERNATIVE TOURISM
A New Paradigm

One type of tourist which has generated a lot of interest among those supporting sustainable development is the alternative tourist described by Krippendorf (1987) as those who try to establish more contact with the local population, try to do without the tourist infrastructure and use the save accommodation and transport facilities as the natives. However, alternative tourism has been criticised as being elitist and spreading tourism to areas that are not yet spoiled by tourism. One who has issued such a warning is Butler (1990, Hawkins, 1994; cited in Theobald, 1997:284). But, in this work much more emphasis has been given on cultural tourism under the theme of adaptancy platform of Jafar Jafari.

The touristic dilemma is clear, to freeze or not to freeze, to maintain boundaries or to remove, to assimilate or to segregate, or in short, the sword cuts with both edges (Jafari, 1984).

Recently, some neighbouring areas outside the Park have been declared as Buffer Zone. The surface area of Buffer Zone is 70,000 ha. This covers whole or portions of a total of 34 VDCs, of which 16 each fall in Nawalparasi and Chitwan districts. A total of 128 village wards are represented in the buffer zone, having a total population of 242,000 (PPP 1997) (KMTNC, 1998:4) Promotion of sustainable tourism in and around the park can improve the living standards of local people. This is especially true for RCNP neighbours because there is a legal mechanism in place to divert 30–35% of park-generated revenue to finance the community development projects in the buffer zone. Some of this annual NRs. 12–20 million plus can be diverted to develop or strengthen tourism infrastructure in the buffer zone, if communities could be persuaded to develop this sector (*ibid*, 8).

Key questions to be considered are: First, how many and what type of tourists does the resident population of an area wish to attract? Second, what is the optimum member of tourists that the area can support in terms of its physical, environmental and social carrying capacity? Third, how can these tourists contribute to the enhancement of the life-styles of the residents?

Planning should be designed to maximise the economic and social benefits of tourism to the resident population, while at the same time mitigating or preferably eliminating the adverse effects. Thoughtful policy-making and planning can do much to minimise or even remove the negative effects.

Given the fact that RCNP's 90% of total revenue is due to tourism activities, and this amount (NRs. 41.5 million in 1994/95) is growing annually by 22.5% (Banskota et al. 1997), the tourism in and around Chitwan must be managed carefully. The haphazard unmanaged tourism growth coupled with the current lessee faire style of park management continues as in the present, it will certainly 'kill the goose that lays the golden eggs'. Some of the ugly signs are already noticeable: According to a recent visitor survey two thirds of the visitors perceived the problem of crowding and congestion in Sauraha and in the park (Banskota et al., 1997). For Sauraha area, it seems to have reached its capacity considering the present level of infrastructure and management. There is a widespread agreement among conservationists that pressure on the park resources in Sauraha due to tourism activities including elephant safari, jungle walk, canoe ride and jungle drive, has already led to habitat degradation of several wildlife species. Increase in land price is encouraging Tharus and other indigenous people to sell their land thereby diminishing the cultural attractions of the area (*ibid*).

If measures to control and limit tourism fail to be taken in the near future, one may expect the national park to come under serious threat. Not only the effects on animal behaviour but also the encroachment on the entire ecosystem need to be given serious consideration (Muller-Boker,1999:57). The Royal Chitwan National Park is experiencing a rising tide of visitors and if the present trend continues, by the end of 2007/08, the tourist number will be about 492,000 which is more than five times greater than the number in 1996/97 (Pradhanang, 1997). These visitors will bring diversified tastes and perhaps would be willing to spend more and may be demanding more services than did the visitors in the past. To fulfill such tastes, one dimension that seems appropriate and can be complementary to nature-based tourism concept would be cultural tourism through reconstructed ethnicity as mentioned earlier. Cultural tourism is closer to the reconstructed ethnicity as mentioned by MacCannell (1984). Local communities should be motivated and trained to take benefit of their potential resources. Tourism plan should be prepared with an aim to benefit local communities. The cultural activities for tourists can include song and dance programs with interpretation, village tours by bullock carts, home visits, interpretation of various village activities, cultural institutions like family, marriage, kinship, socialisation, life-cycle ceremonies, culture and personality, gender role, dresses and ornaments, gastronomy, housing design, village organisation, faith healing pactice, shamanism, symbols, material cultures, festivals, subsistence, myth, legends, folk tales, beliefs, gods and goddess, commensurate rite, religion, rituals, processes, education, interaction with nature, politics and change. The villagers should be encouraged to produce and make handicrafts. The villagers especially would require skill-enhancement opportunities to mobilise local resources to become guides, produce tourism handicraft products and be conversant in travel trade.

In order to develop cultural tourism, it is required to think about cultural tourism demand, cultural motivations for travel, native cultural heritage for tourism, cultural tourism product development, cultural tourism planning and management, cultural tourism marketing and promotion, environmental management for sustaining and promoting cultural tourism, exploring new source markets for cultural tourism, human resource management, cultural organisations and tourism. The rich cultural heritage of the native people holds great promises for creation of 'Special Tourism Areas' for investment, development and marketing which will reduce the burden on existing circuits besides helping tourism industry to face the competition with ease.

After providing the training program to the participants in 1997, the researcher again visited the same place in 1998 and found no interpretation of the native's culture in terms of describing the symbolic meaning of the various cultural items at the time of showing the Tharu stick dance at the Culture House. As one informant reported that its main reason is in the very beginning the information was given to the trainees only about the nature not about the culture of local people in detail as mentioned earlier. Therefore, they could memorise only about the wildlife not about the human's culture. These days due to the tourists' demands each and every lodge owner is showing a keen interest to develop local culture for tourist's attraction. But, unfortunately, the living culture is already dead at the destination. Its alternative will be only the museum culture, as shown in the interest to build a museum by some local entrepreneurs. But, simply constructing a museum house with displaying negligible artifacts will not work for the development of cultural tourism in Sauraha. However, Urry (1991) reckons that it is closely bound up with the post-modern breaking down of boundaries particularly between the front and back stage of people's lives, or what he terms post-modern museum culture in which almost anything can become an object of curiosity to visitors.

Regarding the development of cultural tourism in Sauraha, the researcher had already suggested the development of the living Cultural Center in Chitwan (Pandey *et al.*, 1993:66; Kunwar, 1997:200). But, no concerned authority inquired about the new proposal. When there was a living cultural tradition in Sauraha and its neighbouring areas, no concerned authority and local people showed interest in it. But, now that the culture is getting lost, every one is showing an interest in developing cultural tourism in buffer zone. If cultural tourism is to be developed in buffer zone, there should not be a policy of diversifying the tourist from Sauraha. This is the place where the entrepreneurs have done maximum investment for running hotels. Rather it should have a policy of providing extra 1 day activities to the tourists in an around Sauraha. People of certain parts of Terai have already tasted the importance of tourism and have recognised it as an important industry. Now, Sauraha, without tourism is condemned, with tourism it will be destroyed—the solution: the doctrine of cultural tourism which became the model in Bali, in Indonesia. Cultural tourism would be acceptable for both groups—the hosts and guests. Tourism in Bali is the best model of boundary maintenance. This may happen at a stage of development of tourism when the benefits start percolating to a large section of people and the negative effects of tourism developments are overshadowed by the positive economic gains. The community accepts tourism without any resistance. This process involves establishing a well-defined boundary between the foreign and the local cultures and presenting the local traditions to foreigners in a different context so that the effects of the foreigners on the locals are minimised. Island of Bali is the best example of this kind. The island has kept its cultural traditions and has accepted tourism (Batta, *op. cit.*, 75). This is how Indonesia has developed cultural tourism in Bali. Even the model can be applied at village level in terms of village tourism. If we (Nepalese) want to develop tourism in Nepal we should work ourselves. This is what the Spanish proverb, 'Travelers there are no roads. Roads are made by walking' (Kissinger, 1994) teaches everybody to work on their own. Therefore, for the development of cultural tourism in Chitwan, a different model should be developed there. As proposed earlier in 1993 and 1997, there can be developed Tharu Culture Center (TCC) or Terai Culture Center (TCC) in the live form of representing different Tharu sub-groups of whole Terai or representing the total Teraien cultures (the cultures of different ethnic groups of Terai) in the model of Hawaii (Stanton, 1989) and the model of cultural tourism in Bali, Indonesia (Picard, 1995). Though the model can be borrowed from anywhere, the indigenisational approach should be followed by the planners or policy makers of the destination country. From this kind of development, the tourists length of stay can be increased from 2 nights/3 days to 3 nights/4 days. From this new scheme there will be spillover benifit in the destination area.

'Cultural and environmental pollution' are regarded as the unwelcome accompanying features of modern 'mass tourism' in Nepal. Nearly every travel report includes sentences like destruction of nature caused by tourists from the rich western countries goes hand in hand with destruction of traditional culture (Muller-Boker, 2000:105). It is assumed that maximising the tourist arrivals would bring greater economic benefit to the host destinations. Instead, the often-overlooked truth that tourists are seeking a satisfying experience must be at the centre of any new tourism. Taylor (1994) argues that the success of tourism should not be measured by monetary value alone and factors like image of the destination, the satisfaction level of the visitor, the quality of environment must be included in any measure of success (cited in Batta, 2000:210).

Residents need to adopt and use a tourism ethic. This means that when planning for tourism, residents must consider the social, cultural and environmental consequences of tourism. Tourists too must adopt a tourism ethic—they must consider the social, cultural and environmental consequenccs of their actions. This requires knowledge and tourism education. Tourism education is necessary for the tourist and resident alike. Both need to become more sensitive to each other's needs and culture and to the consequences of being insensitive and unaware (Modi, 2001:134).

REFERENCES

Adams, Kathleen M., 1990, 'Cultural Commoditization in Tana Toraja, Indonesia', *Cultural Survival*, Part 1, Vol. 14, No. 1, pp. 31–34.

Adams, Vincanne, 1992, 'Tourism and Sherpas', *Annals of Tourism Research*, Vol. 19, pp. 534–554.

Archer, Brian, and Chris Cooper, 1997, 'The Positive and Negative Impacts of Tourism', in William F. Theobald (ed.), *Global Tourism: The Next Decade*, Oxford: Buttorworth-Heinemann, pp. 73–91.

Aspelin, P. C., 1977, 'The Anthropological Analysis of Tourism: Indirect Tourism and the Political Economy of the Mamainde of Mato Grosso, Brazil', *Annals of Tourism Research*, Vol. 9 No. 3, pp. 135–160.

Bajracharya, Dayananda, and Vaskar Thapa, 2000, 'King Mahendra Trust for Nature Conservation (KMTNC) and Nature Conservation in Nepal', in Ram Pratap Thapa and Joachim Baaden (eds.), *Nepal Myths and Realities*, Delhi: Book Faith India, pp. 277–306.

Banskota, Kamal, and Bikash Sharma, 1995, *Tourism for Mountain Community Development: Case Study Report on the Annapurna and Gorkha Regions of Nepal.* Kathmandu: CREST.

Batta, R. N., 2000, *Tourism and The Environment: A Quest for Sustainability*, New Delhi: Indus.

Baumgartner, Ruedi, 1986, 'Tourism and Socio-Economic Change: The Case of the Rolwaling Valley in Eastern Nepal', in Klaus Seeland (ed.), *Recent Research on Nepal*, Munchen: Wellform Verlag, pp.199–217.

Beun, Monique, and Anupa Lamichhane, 1999, *Feasibility Study on Village Tourism,* Kathmandu: Action Aid Nepal.

Boissevain, J., 1978, 'Tourism and Development in Malta', *in Tourism and Economic Change: Studies in Third World Societies,* No. 6 , Williamsburg, VA: College of William and Mary, Department of Anthropology.

Boniface, P., and C. Cooper, 1987, *The Geography of Travel and Tourism,* Butterworth: London.

Boorstin, D. J., 1964, *The Image: A Guide to Pseudo-Events in America,* New York: Harper & Row.

Butler, R., 1980, "The Concept of a Tourism Area Cycle of Evolution: Implications for Management of Resources". *Canadian Geographer,* Vol. 24, pp. 5–12.

Butler, R., 1993, 'Pre- and Post-Impact Assessment of Tourism Development', in D. Pearce and R. Butler (eds.), *Tourism Research: Critiques and Challenges,* New York: Routledge, pp. 135–155.

Ceballos-Lascurain, Hector, 1996, *Tourism, Ecotourism and Protected Areas,* IUCN: The World Conservation Union.

Chambers, Erve (ed.), 1997, *Tourism and Culture: An Applied Perspective,* New York: State University Press.

Cleverdon, R., 1979, *The Economic and Social Impact of International Tourism in Developing Countries,* Special Report No. 6, London: Economic Intelligence Unit.

Cohen, Erik, 1972, 'Towards a Sociology of International Tourism', *Sociological Research,* Vol. 39, pp. 164–282.

Cohen, Erik, 1979a, *The Impact of Tourism on the Hill Tribes of Northern Thailand,* Internationales Asienforum 10, pp. 5–38.

Cohen, Erik, 1979b, 'Rethinking the Sociology of Tourism', *Annals of Tourism Research,* Vol. 6 No. 1, pp. 18–35.

Cohen, Erik, 1982, 'Thai Girls and Farang Men', *Annals of Tourism Research,* Vol. 9 No. 3, pp. 403–428.

Cohen, Erik, 1983, 'Insiders and Outsiders: The Dynamic of Bungalow Tourism on the Islands of Southern Thailand', *Human Organization,* Vol. 42, No. 2, pp. 158–162.

Cohen, Erik, 1984, 'The Sociology of Tourism: Approaches, Issues, and Findings', *Annual Review of Sociology,* Vol. 10, pp. 373–392.

Cohen, Erik, (ed.), 1985, 'Tourist Guides', Special Issue of *Annals of Tourism Research,* Vol. 12 No. 1.

Cohen, Erik, 1988, "Traditions in the Qualitative Sociology of Tourism", *Annals of Tourism Research,* Vol. 15, pp. 29–46.

Crick, Malcolm, 1985, 'Tracing the Anthropological Self: Quizzical

Reflections of Field Work, Tourism, and the Ludic', *Social Analysis*, No. 17, pp. 71–92.

Crick, Malcolm, 1989, 'Representations of International Tourism in the Social Sciences: Sun, Sex, Sights, Savings, and Servility', *Annual Review of Anthropology*, Vol. 18, pp. 307–344.

Christaller, W., 1964, 'Some Considerations of Tourism Location of Europe: The Peripheral Regions, Underdeveloped Countries Recreation Areas', *Regional Science Association Papers*, Vol. 12, pp. 95–103.

Daddi, Stephanie, 2001, *Women Guiding Trekkers: In-Roads to A Men's World*, Unpublished Paper Submitted at Cornell Nepal Study Program.

Dann, Graham, 2000, "Theoretical Advances in the Sociological Treatment of Tourism," in Stella R. Quah and Arnand Sales *(eds.) The International Handbook of Sociology*, London: SAGE, pp. 367-366.

Dann, Graham M.S., 1997, 'Tourism: The Nostalgia Industry of the Future', pp. 55–68.

Davidson, Rob, 1989, *Tourism*, Pitman.

Davidson, Thomas Lea, 1997, 'What are Travel and Tourism: Are They Really an Industry?', in William F. Theobald (ed.), *Global Tourism: The Next Decade*, Oxford: Butterworth-Heinemann, pp. 20–26.

Deitch, Lewis I., 1989, 'The Impact of Tourism on the Arts and Crafts of the Indians of the Southwestern United States', in Valen L. Smith (ed.), *Hosts and Guests: The Anthropology of Tourism*, Philadelphia: University of Pennsylvania Press, pp. 221–235.

Dhar, Renu S., 1993, *Strategies for Tourism Promotion in India: Some Reflections and Perspectives for the Future*, Unpublished M.Phil Dissertation Submitted to Indian Institute of Public Administration, Delhi.

Dogan, H. Z., 1989, 'Forms of Adjustment: Sociocultural Impacts of Tourism', *Annals of Tourism Research*, Vol. 16, pp. 216–236.

Donnell, Mike Ó, 1992, *A New Introduction to Sociology*, Surry: Thomas Nelson and Sons Ltd.

Doxey, G. V., 1975, 'A Causation Theory of Visitors--Resident Irritants: Methodology and Research Influence', *in Proceedings of the Travel Research Associates 6th Annual Conference*, San Diego, California, pp. 195–198.

Eckerd, Stephen T.,1979, 'Baskets of Nepal', *Pacific Discovery*, Vol. XXXIII, No.1, pp.12–18.

Eshleman, J. Ross, and Barbara G. Cashion, 1983, *Sociology*, Boston and Toronto: Little, Brown and Company.

Fisher, James, 1990, *Reflections on Change in Himalayan Nepal*, New Delhi: Oxford University Press.

Forster, John, 1964, 'The Sociological Consequences of Tourism', *International Journal of Comparative Sociology*, Vol. 5, pp. 217–227.

Friedmann, M., 1992, *A Theory of the Consumption Function*, Princeton: Princeton University Press.

Getz, Donald, 1997, 'Event Tourism and the Authenticity Dilemma', in William F. Theobald (ed.), *Global Tourism: The next decade*, Oxford: Butterworth-Heinemann, pp. 313–329.

Gilbert, D. C., 1990, 'Conceptual Issues in the Meaning of Tourism', in C. P. Cooper (ed.), *Progress in Tourism, Recreation and Hospitality Management*, London Belhaven Press, Vol. II, pp. 1–27.

Gilpin, Alan, 1973, *Dictionary of Economic Terms*, London: Butterworth.

Goffman, Erving, 1959, *The Presentation of Self in Everyday Life*, Garden City, NY: Doubleday.

Graburn, N. H., 1967, 'The Eskimos and 'Airport Art' *Trans-action* (October), pp. 28–33.

Graburn, N. H., 1976, *Ethnic and Tourist Arts: Cultural Expressions From the Fourth World*, California: University of California Press, pp. 1-32.

Graburn, N. H., 1983a, 'The Anthropology of Tourism', *Annals of Tourism Research*, Vol. 10, No. 1, pp. 9–33.

Graburn, N. H., 1983b, 'To Pray, Pay and Play: The Cultural Structure of Japanese Domestic Tourism', Unpublished Paper Collected from SOAS, London.

Graburn, Nelson H. H., 1989, "Tourism: The Sacred Journey," in Valene L. Smith *(ed.) Hosts and Guests: The Anthropology of Tourism* Philadelphia: University of Pennsylvania Press, pp. 21-36.

Graburn, Nelson H. H., and Roland S. Moore, 1994, 'Anthropological Research on Tourism', in J. R. Ritchie and C. Goeldner (eds.), *Travel, Tourism and Hospitality*, Wiley, pp. 233-242.

Greenwood, Davydd J, 1972, 'Tourism as an Agent of Change', *Ethnology*, Vol. xi, pp. 80–91.

Greenwood, Davydd J, 1989, 'Culture by the Pound: An

Anthropological Perspective on Tourism as Cultural Commoditization', in Valene L. Smith (ed.), *Hosts and Guests: The Anthropology of Tourism*, Philadelphia: University of Pennsylvania Press, pp. 171-186.

Guneratne, Arjun, 1994, *The Tharus of Chitwan: Ethnicity, Class and the State in Nepal,* Unpublished PhD Thesis, University of Chicago, Illinois.

Guneratne, Arjun, 1999, 'The Modernising Matwalis: Caste, Class and Status among the Tharus of Chitwan', in Harald O. Skar (ed.), *Nepal:Tharu and Tarai Neighbours,* Kathmandu: EMR, pp. 159–173.

Gunn, C. A., 1994, *Tourism Planning,* 3rd edn., Washington, DC: Taylor and Francis.

Gurung, C. P., and M. De Coursey, 1994, 'The Annapurna Conservation Area Project: A Pioneering Example of Sustainable Tourism?' in Erlet Cater and Gwen Lowman (eds.), *Ecotourism: A Sustainable Option*?, New York: Wiley, pp. 177–194.

Gurung, Dibya, 1995, *Tourism and Gender Impact and Implications of Tourism an Nepalese Women,* Kathmandu: ICIMOD.

Gurung, K. K., 1983, *Heart of the Jungle: The Wildlife of the Chitwan, Nepal,* London.

Herskovits, Melville J., 1938, *Acculturation: The Study of Culture Contact,* New York: J. J. Augustin.

Hirschmann, A. O., 1958, *The Strategy of Economic Development,* New Haven: Yale University Press.

HMG Ministry of Culture, Tourism and Civil Aviation, 2000, *Annual Statistical Report,* Kathmandu.

IUCN, 1993, *Nature Reserves of the Himalaya and the Mountains of Central Asia,* New Delhi.

Jackson, Ian, 1989, *An Introduction to Tourism,* Melbourne: Hospitality Press.

Jafari, Jafar, 1984, 'Unbounded Ethnicity: The Tourist Network and Its Satellites', *Revue de Tourisme,* Vol. 3, pp. 4–21.

Jefferson, A., and L. Lickorish,1988, *Marketing Tourism—A Practical Guide,* Essex: Longman.

Kariel, Herbert G., and Dianne L. Draper, 1995, 'Outdoor Recreation and Tourism in Mountain Environments', in N. J. R. Allen (ed.), *Mountain At Risk,* New Delhi: Manohar, pp. 220–237.

Kermath, B. H., and R. N. Thomas, 1992, 'Spatial Dynamics of

Resorts: Sosuwa, Dominican Republic,' *Annals of Tourism Research,* Vol. 29, pp. 173–190.

Khan, M. M.,1997, 'Tourism Development and Dependency Theory: Mass Tourism vs Ecotourism', *Annals of Tourism Research,* Vol. 32, No.1.

King Mahendra Trust for Nature Conservation, 1996, *Royal Chitwan National Park After Twenty Years: An Assisment of Values, Threats and Opportunities,* Chitwan: KMTNC.

King Mahendra Trust for Nature Conservation, 1998, *Buffer Zone Policy Analysis of the Royal Chitwan National Park,* Technical Report , Chitwan: KMTNC.

Kissinger, Henry, 1994, *Diplomacy,* New York: Simon & Schuster.

Krippendorf, J. 1986, 'The New Tourism', *Tourism Management,* Vol. 7, No. 2, London, pp. 131–5.

Kumar, Ravi Bhushan, 1995, *Coastal Tourism and Environment,* New Delhi: APH Publishing Corporation.

Kunwar, Ramesh Raj, 1989, *Fire of Himal: An Anthropological Study of the Sherpas of Nepal Himalayan Region,* Jaipur: Nirala Publications.

Kunwar, Ramesh Raj, 1997b, *Tourism and Development Science and Industry Interface,* Kathmandu: Laxmi Kunwar.

Lanfant, Marie-Franacoise, 1993, 'Methodological and Conceptual Issues Raised by the Study of International Tourism', in D. Pearce and R. Butler (eds.), *Tourism Research: Critiques and Challenges,* New York: Routledge and Kegan Paul, pp. 70–87.

Lanfant, Marie-Francoise, John B. Allcock, and Edward M. Bruner (eds.), 1995, *International Tourism: Identity and Change,* London: Sage.

Larkey, Edward, 1994, *Pungent Sounds. Constructing Identity with Popular Music in Austria,* New York: Peter Lang.

Lea, John, 1988, *Tourism and Development in the Third World,* London: Routledge.

Leiper, N.,1979, 'The Framework of Tourism', *Annals of Tourism Research.*

Lett, J., 1987, *The Human Enterprise: A Critical Introduction to Anthropological Theory,* Boulder, CO: Westview Press.

Lewis, C. C., and R. E. Chamder, 1989, *Marketing Leadership in Hospitality,* New York: Van Nostrand Reinhold.

Lindberg, K., & J. Enriquez, 1994, *An Analysis of Ecotourism's Economic Contribution to Conservation and Development in Belize,* 2 Vol., Washington, DC: World Wildlife Fund.

Luger, Kurt, 2000, *Kids of Khumbu*, Kathmandu: Mandal Book Point.

Luger, Patricia East Kurt, and Karin Inmann (eds.), 1998, *Sustainability in Mountain Tourism*, Delhi: Book Faith India.

MacCannell, D., 1973, 'Staged Authenticity Arrangements of Social Space in Tourist Settings', *American Journal of Sociology*, Vol. 79, No. 3, pp. 589-603.

MacCannell, D., 1984, 'Reconstructed Ethnicity: Tourism and Cultural Identity in Third World Communities', *Annals of Tourism Research*, Vol. 11, pp. 375–391.

MacCannell, D., 1992, *Empty Meeting Grounds*, New York: Routledge and Kegan Paul.

Mathieson, Alister, and Geoffrey Wall, 1982, *Tourism: Economic Physical and Social Impact*, London: Longman.

McIntosh, R. W., 1977, *Tourism: Principles, Practices and Philosophies*, Ohio: Grid Inc. Columbus.

McKean, Philip, 1976, 'Tourism, Culture Change and Culture Conservation in Bali', in D. J. Banks (ed.), *Changeing Identities in Modern Southeast Asia*, The Hague: Mouton, pp. 237–248.

McKean, Philip, 1989, 'Towards a Theoretical Analysis of Tourism: Economic Dualism and Cultural Involution in Bali', in Valene L. Smith (ed.), *Hosts and Guests: The Anthropology of Tourism*, Philadelphia: University of Pennsylvania Press, pp. 119-138.

McLean, Joanne, 1997–98, Conservation, Relocation and Cultural Survival of the Tharu of Chitwan around the Royal Chitwan National Park, Nepal, Progress Report Submitted to Research Division, Tribhuvan University, Kirtipur, Nepal.

Mead, Margaret, 1932, *The Changing Culture of an Indian Tribe*, New York: Columbia University.

Michaud, J., 1991, 'A Social Anthropology of Tourism in Ladakh, India', *Annals of Tourism Research*, Vol. 19, pp. 191–212.

Mikame, Kiyotomi, 1979, 'A Note on the Faguwa Festival of Chitwan Tharu', *Kailash*, Vol. VII, No. 3, pp. 226–246.

Milne, S. S., 1987, 'Differential Multipliers', *Annals of Tourism Research*, Vol. 14, No. 4, pp. 499–515.

Mishra, Hemanta R., and Margeret Jefferies, 1991, *Royal Chitwan National Park: Wildlife Heritage of Nepal*, Kathmandu: King Mahendra Trust for Nature Conservation.

Modi, Shalini, 2001, *Tourism and Society Cross Cultural Perspectives*, New Delhi: Rawat Publications.

Moore, J. D.,1997, *Visions of Culture: An Introduction to*

Anthropological Theories and Theorists, New Delhi: Sage.

Muller-Boker, Ulrike, 1999, *The Chitawan Tharus in Southern Nepal, An Ethnoecological* (Translated by Philip Piarce), Stuttgart: Franz Steiner Verlag.

Muller-Boker, Ulrike, 2000, 'Ecotourism in Nepal: The example of the Royal Chitwan National Park', in Ram Pratap Thapa and Joachim Baaden (eds.), *Nepal Myths and Realities*, Delhi: Book Faith India, pp. 100–118.

Muller, Hansruedi, 2001, "Tourism and Hospitality into the 21st Century," in A Lockwood and S. Medlik (*eds.*) *Tourism and Hospitality in the 21st Century*, Oxford: Butterworth, pp. 61-70.

Nash, Dennison, 1981, 'Tourism as an Anthropological Subject', *Current Anthropology*, Vol. 22, No. 5, pp. 461–481.

Nash, Dennison, 1984, 'The Ritualization of Tourism: Comment on Graburn's 'The Anthropology of Tourism', *Annals of Tourism Research*, Vol. 11, No. 3, pp. 503–507.

Nash, Dennison, 1996, *Anthropology of Tourism*, Oxford: Pergamon.

Nepal, Sanjay K., 1997, 'Sustainable Tourism, Protected Areas, and Livelihood Needs of Local Communities in Developing Countries', *International Journal of Sustainable Development, World Ecology*, Vol. 4, No. 2, pp. 123-134.

Nicholls, L. L., 1976, 'Tourism and Crime', *Annals of Tourism Research*, Vol. 3, pp. 176–82.

Nielsen, Christian, 2001, *Tourism and the Meida*, Melbourne: Hospitality Press.

Noronha, R.,1973, *A Report on the Proposed Tourism Project, Bali*, Washington: IBRD.

Noronha, R., 1977a, *Social and Cultural Dimansions of Tourism: A Review of the Literature in English*, Draft Working Paper, World Bank, New York.

Noronha, R., 1977b, Social and Cultural Dimensions of Tourism: A Review of the Literature in English, Washington, DC: World Bank (Draft).

Noronha, R., 1979, 'Paradise Reviewed: Tourism in Bali', in de Kadt Emannuel (ed.), *Tourism Passport to Development*, New York: Oxford University Press, pp. 177–204.

Nunez, Theron A., 1963, 'Tourism, Tradition and Acculturation: Weekendismo in a Mexican village', *Ethnology*, Vol. II, No.3, pp. 347–352.

Nunez, Theron A., 1989, 'Touristic Studies in Anthropological Perspective', in V. L. Smith (ed.), *Hosts and Guests: The*

Anthropology of Tourism, Philadelphia: University of Pennsylvania Press, pp. 207–216.

Oppermann, M. 1993, 'Tourism Space in Developing Countries', *Annals of Tourism Research*, Vol. 20, pp. 535–556.

Pandey, Ram, Niwas, Pitambar Chettri, Ramesh Raj Kunwar, and Govinda Ghimire, 1993, *Effects of Tourism on Culture and Environment in Nepal*, Kathmandu: UNESCO.

Pearce, P., 1982, *The Social Psychology of Tourist Behaviour*, Oxford: Peramon Press.

Pearce, P., 1997, 'Tourism–Resident Impacts: Examples, Explanations and Emerging Solutions', in William F. Theobald (ed.), *Global Tourism: The Next Decade*, Oxford: Butterworth-Heinemann, pp. 103–123.

Peck, John Gregory, and Alice Shear Lepie, 1989, 'Tourism and Development in Three North Carolina Coastal Towns', in V. L. Smith (ed.), *Hosts and Guests: The Anthropology of Tourism*, Philadelphia: University of Pennsylvania Press, pp. 203–222.

Picard, Michael, 1995, 'Cultural Heritage and Tourist Capital: Cultural Tourism in Bali', in Marie-Francoise Lamfant, John B. Allock, and Edward M. Bruner (eds.), *International Tourism: Identity and Change*, Sage, pp. 44–66.

Plog, S.C., 1972, "Why Destination Areas Rise and Fall in their Popularity," Plog Association, San Francisco, USA.

Pradhan, I. K., 1979, *Nepalese Tourism in Perspectives*, Kathmandu: Nepal Research Group.

Pradhan, Kamal Maiya, 1997, *Planning Tourism in Nepal*, New Delhi: Vikas Publishing House.

Pradhan, Kamal Maiya, 1998, 'A Survey of Concepts and Theories of Tourism', *The Himalayan Review*, Vol. xxix, pp. 1–9.

Price, Martin F., 1995, 'Patterns of the Development of Tourism in Mountain Communities', in N. J. R. Allen (ed.), *Mountain At Risk*, New Delhi: Manohar, pp. 199–219.

Pronovost, Gilles, 2000, "The Collapse of the Leisure Society? New Channenges for the Sociology of Leisure," in Stella R. Quah and Arnaud Sales (*eds.*), *The International Handbook of Sociology*, London: SAGE, pp. 356-366.

Pyakuryal, Kailash,1982, *Ethnicity and Rural Development: A Sociological Study of Four Tharu Villages in Chitwan Nepal*, PhD Thesis, Michigan State University.

Pye, E., and T. B. Lin, 1983, *Tourism in Asia: The Economic Impact, Singapore:* Singapore University Press.

Reime, Man, and Hawkins Cameron, 1980, 'Planning and the

Developing Hospitality Facilites that Increase Tourism Demand', in Donald E. Hawkins, Elwood L. Shafer, and James M. Rovelstad (eds.), *Tourism Marketing and Management Issues*, Washington: George Washington University Press.

RESOURCES NEPAL, 1999, *Protected Areas of Nepal.*

Ritchie, J. R., and M. Zins, 1978, 'Culture as a Determinant of the Attractiveness of a Tourist Region', *Annals of Tourism Research*, Vol. 5, pp. 252–267.

Ritcher, Linda K., 1989 (Reprinted 2000), *The Politics of Tourism*, New Delhi: Manohar.

Rodenberg , Eric E.,1980, 'The Effects of Scale in Economic Development: Tourism in Bali', *Annals of Tourism Research*, Vol. 7, No. 2, pp. 177–196.

Rogers, Everett, 1983, *Diffusion of Innovations*, New York.

Rogers, Paul, and John Aitchision, 1998, *Towards Sustainable Tourism in the Everest Region*, Kathmandu: IUCN.

Rostow, W., 1960, *The Stages of Economic Growth*, Cambridge: Cambridge University Press.

Sapkota, Krishana, 2000, 'Mass Tourism vs. Eco-Tourism in Sauraha', *The Wildlife*, No. 3.

Satyal, Yajna Raj, 1999, *Tourism in Nepal: A Profile*, Delhi: Adroit Publishers.

Satyal, Yajna Raj, 2000a, *Essentials of Tourism*, Delhi: Adroit Publishers.

Satyal, Yajna Raj, 2000b, *Tourism Monograph of Nepal*, Delhi: Adroit Publishers.

Schiffman, I., 1989, *Alternative Techniques for Managing Growth*, California: Institute of Government Studies, University of California at Berkeley.

Schneider, Peter Jane Schneider, and Edward Hansen, 1972, 'Modernization and Development: The Role of Regional Elites and Noncorporate Groups in the European Mediterranean', *Comparative Studies in Society and History*, Vol. 14, pp. 328-350.

Schneider, Susan C., and Jean-Louis Barsoux, 1997, *Managing Across Cultures*, London: Prentice- Hall.

Sharma, Pitamber, 1995a, *A Framework for Tourism Carrying Capacity, Analysis*, Kathmandu: ICIMOD.

Sharma, Pitamber, (ed.), 2000, *Tourism as Development: Case Studies from the Himalaya*, Lalitpur: Himal Books.

Sharma, Prayag Raj, 1995b, *Culture and Tourism: Defining Roles and Relationship,* Kathmandu: ICIMOD.

Sharp, Lauriston, 1952, 'Steel Axes for Stone-Age Australians', *Human Organization,* Vol. 11, pp. 17–22.

Shrestha, Tej Kumar, 1994, *Encounter with the Himalayan Wildlife,* Kathmandu: Bimala Shrestha.

Shrestha, Tirtha Bahadur, 1995, *Mountain Tourism and Environment in Nepal,* Kathmandu: ICIMOD.

Shrestha, Tirtha Bahadur, 1999, *Nepal Country Report on Biological Diversity,* Kathmandu: IUCN.

Shivji, I. (ed.), 1973, *Tourism and Socialist Development, Dar-es-Salaam,* Tanzania Publishing House.

Sinclair, M. T., 1998, 'Tourism and Economic Development: A Survey', *The Journal of Development Studies,* Vol. 34, No. 5, pp. 1–49.

Singh, T. V., 1989, *The Kullu Valley: Impact of Tourism Development in Mountain Areas,* New Delhi: Himalayan Publication.

Smith, S. L. J., 1994, 'The Tourism Product', *Annals of Tourism Research,* Vol. 21, No. 2, pp. 582–595.

Smith, Valene L.,1980, 'Anthropology and Tourism: A Science–Industry Evaluation', *Annals of Tourism Research,* Vol. VII, No. 1, pp.13–33.

Smith, Valene L., 1981, 'Controlled vs. Uncontrolled Tourism: Bhutan and Sikkim', *Rain,* Vol. 40, pp. 4–6.

Smith, Valene L., (ed.), 1989, *Hosts and Guests: The Anthropology of Tourism,* Philadelphia: University of Pennsylvania Press.

Srinivas, M. N., 1965, *Social Change in Modern India,* Berkeley: University of California Press.

Stanton, Max E., 1989, 'The Polynesian Cultural Center: A Multi-Ethnic Model of Seven Pacific Cultures', in Valene L. Smith (ed.), *Hosts and Guests: The Anthropology of Tourism,* Philadelphia: University of Pennsylvania Press, pp. 247-262.

Stevens, Stan, 1997, 'Annapurna Conservation Area: Empowerment and Development in Nepal', in Stan Steven (ed.), *Conservation through Survival,* Washington, DC: Island Press, pp. 237–261.

Swain, M. B., 1977, 'Cuna Women and Ethnic Tourism: A Way to Persist and an Avenue to Change', in Valene L. Smith (ed.), *Hosts and Guests: The Anthropology of Tourism,* Philadelphia: University of Pennsylvania Press, pp. 71–82.

Swinglehurst, Edmund, 1997, 'Face-to-face: The Socio-cultural Impacts of Tourism', in William F. Theobald (ed.), *Global*

Tourism: The Next Decade, Oxford: Butterworth-Heinimann, pp. 92–102.

Theobald, William, F., 1997, 'The Context, Meaning and Scope of Tourims', in William F. Theobald (ed.), *Global Tourism: The Next Decade,* Butterworth, pp. 3–19.

Turner, L., and J. Ash, 1975, *The Golden Hordes: International Tourism and the Pleasure Periphery,* London: Constable.

Turner, V., 1973, 'The Center Out There: Pilgrim's Goal,' *History of Religions,* Vol. 12, pp. 191–230.

Urry, J., 1991, *The Tourist Gaze,* London: Sage.

Vallee, P., 1987, *Authenticity as a Factor in Segmenting the Canadian Travel Market,* Master's Thesis, Department of Recreation and Leisure Studies, University of Waterloo.

Wagner, U., 1977, 'Out of Time and Place: Mass Tourism and Charter Trips', *Ethnos,* Vol. 42, No. 1/2, pp. 38-52.

Wahab, S. E., 1971, *Tourism Management,* London: International Tourism Press.

Wahnschafft, R., 1982, 'Formal and Informal Tourism Sectors: A Case Study in Pattaya', *Annals of Tourism Research,* Vol. 9, pp. 429–451.

Wallerstein, Immanuel, 1974, *The Modern World-System: Capitalist Agriculture and the Origins of the European World-Economy in the Sixteenth Century,* New York: Academic Press.

Warner, Wilson, Larry Dennis, and Allen P. Wadsworth Jr., 1976, 'Authoritarianism Left and Right', *Bullentin of the Psychonomic Society,* Vol. 7, pp. 271–274.

Weiler, Betty, 2001, "Tourism Research and Theories: A Review," in A. Lockwood and S. Medlik (*eds.*) *Tourism and Hospitality in the 21st Century,* Oxford: Butterworth, pp. 94-105.

Wells, M. P., 1993, 'Neglect of Biological Riches: The Economics of Nature Tourism in Nepal' *Biodiverrsity and Conservation,* Vol. 2, pp. 445–464.

Wilson, D., 1979, 'The Early Effects of Tourism on the Seychelles', in Emannuel de Kadt (ed.), *Tourism Passport to Development,* New York: Oxford University Press, pp. 205–236.

Wolf, Eric, 1982, *Europe and the People Without History,* Berkeley, CA: University of California Press.

Yonzon, Prasanna, 2000, 'Habitat Fragmentation', *The Wildlife,* No. 4, pp. 57–59.

Young, G., 1973, *Tourism: Blessing or Blight*? Harmondsworth: Penguin Books.

Royal Chitwan National Park is the third Tourist Destination of Nepal.

A View of One Horn Rhino in the Chitwan Park.

A view of Male Sambar Deer.

The Tourists with the Native of Sauraha.

In 1970s and mid-80s, there were almost these kinds of Tharu Huts which were Providing Accommodation to the Tourists.

The Tharu Hut is being Gradually Replaced by the Modern Buildings. A View of the Hotels at the same came in two Variables.

A View of Luxurious Hotel Hermitage Boat House under Construction.

The Tharu Stick Dance is one of the most important Products of Sauraha.

The Tourists are just getting out of Hotel for Village Tour.

The Tourists will make a visit to this kind of Tharu Habitat.

The typical Tharu house of Padampur Village.

Tourists crossing the river near Sauraha.
They are on the way back from Village Tour.

In almost Village Tour, the Hoteliers provide Oxen or Bullock Cart to the Tourists. A view of Oxen Cart Crossing the River.

Cart Drive is another important part in Sauraha.

An elevated house for over night stay inside the Jungle.
The is newly innovated tented camp inside the community forest.

The elephant ride is considered as one of the most important activities inside and outside the Chitwan Park.

Jungle drive is another important activity inside and outside the Chitwan Park.

There are many watch towers (known as *machan*) inside the jungle. The tourists stop their jeep and watch the animals from watch tower.

A view of making bicycle tour in Sauraha.

A View of Elephant Mating.

A view of Rhino Mating.

Courtesy: Madhav Lal Maharjan

The Tharu girls of Chitwan.

The Tharu girls of Morang.

The Tharu girls of Kailali.

The Tharu festival held in Chitwan on the occasion of Visit Nepal 1998.

The Tharu Basketry.

The Chitwaniya Tharu's traditional ornaments.